The junior church programme with a difference!

Three + One
From trouble to triumph

Michael Forster

Kevin Mayhew

First published in 2000 by
KEVIN MAYHEW LTD
Buxhall
Stowmarket
Suffolk IP14 3BW

© 2000 Michael Forster

The right of Michael Forster to be identified as the author of this work
has been asserted by him in accordance with the Copyright, Designs
and Patents Act 1988.

The worksheets and dramas may be photocopied by the purchasing church
without copyright infringement, provided they are used for the purpose
for which they are intended. Reproduction of any of the contents of this
book for commercial purposes is subject to the usual copyright restrictions.

No other part of this publication may be reproduced, stored in a retrieval system,
or transmitted, in any form or by any means, electronic, mechanical, photocopying,
recording or otherwise, without the prior written permission of the publisher.

All rights reserved.

0 1 2 3 4 5 6 7 8 9

ISBN 1 84003 642 7
Catalogue No 1500388

Cover design by Jonathan Stroulger
Illustrated by Simon Smith
Edited by Katherine Laidler
Typesetting by Louise Selfe
Printed in Great Britain

Contents

Foreword	5
Introduction	7
How to get the best from this book	9

Unit 1: The story of Joseph

Overview of the unit	16
Week 1: Joseph is sold into slavery	17
Week 2: Joseph is imprisoned	25
Week 3: Joseph becomes governor of Egypt	31
Week 4: All-age worship	39

Unit 2: Israel in Babylon – from military defeat to moral victory

Overview of the unit	44
Week 1: Shadrach, Meshach and Abednego	45
Week 2: The king learns that pride goes before a fall	53
Week 3: Daniel in the lions' den	59
Week 4: All-age worship	67

Unit 3: Jesus – from despair to hope

Overview of the unit	72
Week 1: Simeon's vigil of hope and prayer	73
Week 2: Lazarus is called back to life	79
Week 3: Jesus appears to his disciples at Emmaus	87
Week 4: All-age worship	93

*This series of books is dedicated to the worshippers of
all ages at my own church in Anstey, Leicestershire,
with gratitude for their openness and enthusiasm
in field-testing and developing this concept.*

*Special thanks are due to
Laura Doody and Claire Pearson
for their help with the proof-reading.*

Foreword

This series of books takes what might to many people seem to be a new approach to Junior Church teaching and all-age worship. In fact, though, it's a very old one – used, according to the Gospels, by Jesus himself.

First and foremost, Jesus valued people, cared about them, was concerned for their needs. He called people to become part of a community where they – many of them for the first time – were valued and enabled to feel that they were part of something worthwhile, that their lives had meaning and purpose. In the course of that, they learned a great deal and their commitment to Jesus and what he stood for grew until in many cases it was a life-commitment in more ways than one.

So the approach we take here is to focus on building relationships – including the children in something they may come to value, telling the faith story in engaging ways and letting the 'learning' be a spin-off benefit. I am convinced that that is a more effective way of working with children than focusing just on the imparting of knowledge.

People often complain that youth organisations do not seem 'interested in the Church'. The reality is that there is no *reason* for them to be interested: without faith commitment there is no other point in going to church when everything else it offers can be had more easily and more satisfyingly elsewhere. And that faith commitment will, I believe, be built more effectively, in their early years, by making them part of something they value *because it values them* rather than by trying to teach them things.

That brings me to the vital difference that sets this material apart. The sessions are arranged in sets of four: three 'Junior Church' sessions building into an all-age service on the fourth Sunday when the children's work will be celebrated and valued by the whole Church fellowship, and the adults will have the opportunity to learn both from and with the children.

I hope and pray that these resources will open minds of all ages to the wonder of God's love and the joy of sharing it, rather than merely fill them up with doctrines and ethical propositions.

All that will follow. The first thing – and the vital thing – is to *relate*.

Enjoy the book. Enjoy one another. Oh, and enjoy God, of course!

MICHAEL FORSTER

Introduction
(Please read this – I think you're going to like it!)

This series of books arose out of a particular need. We were finding the usual age-based 'classes' difficult to sustain in our context, and mixed-age groups seemed the only option – but the cry went up, 'You can't teach five- and ten-year-olds in the same class' (I'll have more to say about the 'teaching' idea later).

At the same time, we wanted to include the children much more in the actual planning of our monthly all-age worship which, until then, tended to be a bit of a one-man show that was done *for* rather than *with* them. But just when do you gather increasingly busy and pressurised children together to plan services?

This is what we decided to do. We would take an overall theme that could be presented in three weekly stories, and the learning process would consist of fun activities: story-telling, art and craft, drama, music, some of which could then become the basis for the all-age service. But what if some children could only come for two of the weeks? Would they be left out? Clearly, each week's story, while relating to the three-week theme, would need to be able to stand alone.

Wouldn't it make the all-age worship terribly long and overladen with material? Probably, if *all* the previous three-weeks' work were used – so the Junior Church would choose just one of the three stories as the focus for the service, but let the worship leader put it into context with the help of the pictures, models, etc., that the children had made. That would enable most of the art and craftwork to be on display in the church, providing a visual background to the storytelling. And storytelling really is the basis of communicating our faith. Ask any of our Jewish cousins! Or ask Jesus!

So this material was written, and some of it has been used, and the basic idea and format have been tried and tested. One exciting result has been the releasing of some previously unrecognised creativity as children who had not been in the limelight before took the basic ideas and developed them in wonderfully imaginative ways. In the very first month of using this material, we discovered some real hidden treasure – and we did so in worship where we could properly celebrate and give thanks for it.

And that brings me to the most important thing we learned from this. Don't let the all-age worship become a talking shop! The discussion-type activities will quickly lose their appeal if that happens. We saw this coming in good time and proposed the setting up of a Worship and Mission Action Group (definitely *not* a committee) within the church to carry forward some of the ideas that come out of these sessions. Such a group must be a 'ginger group' rather than a management committee. They should not get bogged down in the minutiae of keeping new projects going, but simply research ideas and present possibilities to the relevant meetings (more than once if necessary!) to ensure that they are not simply lost in a sea of good intentions. If that were to happen – if the cards, etc., that the discussion groups produce were simply thrown away or filed and forgotten, we think it would not be long before the worship became stale: 'Oh, another of those silly discussions, again.' However, if the action group is set up, and enabled to work well, the all-age worship could become a real source of inspiration for the Church's mission – something through which the Holy Spirit might breathe renewal into the Church and the local community.

How to get the best from this book

The book is based on three 'units', each of which is a four-week cycle: three Junior Church sessions, and one all-age worship. Those Churches that currently have a monthly 'family service' will find it best to plan so that the 'fourth' Sunday in each unit falls on whatever Sunday of the month is appropriate for their system. (When there are five Sundays, that's not a problem – you'll appreciate the extra time to pull the threads together all the more firmly ready for the all-age service.)

Each session divides into a number of activities, and a worksheet is also provided either to do in the session or as a take-home resource. There will almost certainly be too much here for the single session of perhaps 45 minutes that most Junior Churches have – so *don't think you have to use it all*. (Nothing destroys a good learning environment like trying to cram too much in!) Choose what you think best fits your group in each particular case, and perhaps have other items standing by in case you run out. Much of course will depend on the number of children you have. A small Junior Church could work all together, concentrating on the story and just one or two activities, whereas a large one might start together for the storytelling and then break up into several multi-age groups, each focusing on a different activity – some children producing art and craft work, others doing drama, learning new songs, etc.

Similarly, you don't need necessarily to use all of sessions one to three. You may decide, in particular circumstances, to omit one session and spread the other two over the three weeks. The stories are written as stand-alone units, so you can do this quite easily. At the risk of labouring the point, the all-age worship in Week Four should be a celebration of whatever has been done – not a goal to be striven for and which becomes a blight on the sessions because the children are under pressure.

Most importantly of all, remember the central aims: the session should:

- be enjoyable for all concerned
- make all the children feel valued and cared about
- contribute to building relationships.

If you do these things, then the 'teaching' will happen, because children are great learners if the environment is right. They'll virtually teach themselves!

Let's have a look at each of the elements that comprise the sessions.

Thinking about it

This is vital – the advance preparation need not be unduly time-consuming or tedious, but it will transform the actual session. In fact, we found that the preparation required in using this material was much less onerous than preparing traditional lessons.

- A monthly meeting of key people would be a good idea, perhaps after Week Three, when you can pull together the all-age service and look ahead to the next four weeks.

- Decide which week's subtheme will form the basis of the all-age worship. You need to know this at the outset so that you will know which week's 'ticked' activity to prepare and which you can ignore.
- Then each week look through the relevant session thoroughly and give some thought to which would be the most appropriate and helpful elements to concentrate on, in your situation.
- Prepare any resources: art/craft materials, visual aids, legitimate photocopies, etc., that you need. Try to anticipate the kinds of questions the children might ask – or that you could helpfully ask them.

What's the point?

It's helpful to have a specific point in mind that we wish to convey. This does not mean we can't find other things in the text, but one point retained is better than five confused or forgotten – and more likely to engage the children's attention, too! They have the rest of their lives to explore the countless layers of meaning, so don't let's spoil it by cramming them too full of rich food!

Now for the session itself.

Doing it

Prayer

An opening prayer is offered. However, we should be careful about stereotyping prayer too much as merely 'talking to God'. It might be worth thinking about encouraging children to think of prayer as consciously *being with* God – sometimes quietly, but also in the more active parts of life. So let God join in the activities, the fun, most of all in the growing *relationships* between staff, parents and children. In a different kind of way, the whole session is 'prayer' – and both kinds are important.

For this reason, the prayers are short and are all focused in such a way as to point the children to that greater reality: the unconditional love of God.

From the known to the unknown

Jesus understood well the first principle of teaching: begin with what people know, and only then introduce the new. His most effective teaching, according to the Gospel records, was in parables. Often, he simply didn't mention scripture at all.

That is not an argument against biblical teaching – rather it is a plea to make it more effective. Children are wonderful at making connections – much better than we adults with our 'disciplined' (trammelled?) minds. So we begin by appealing to what they know, and then tell them the biblical story. With little or no prompting, they often will then grasp joyfully and spontaneously for themselves what we so often labour painfully and ineffectually to drill into them – and no one's more guilty of that than I am!

Tell the story

Story-telling is the basis of keeping the faith alive. Our Jewish forebears kept their children in the faith by telling and retelling vibrant stories, often around meal-tables, camp fires or in other informal settings, with plenty of song and laughter to help it along. So a child-friendly version of a Bible story is the mainstay of each week's material. It's a good idea to read it a few times in advance, so you are familiar and can half-tell, half-read it to the children with plenty of eye contact and other interaction. Or you can get them to tell it to each other by acting it out – see 'Drama', below. You may also find it useful to have some visual aids handy, or think of some questions you can ask, breaking off from the narrative whenever you choose to ask, 'How do you think God felt about that?' 'What d'you think happened then?' 'What would you have done about that?' etc. This will all help to maintain the children's interest – with a little imagination you can easily keep them enthralled!

Respond to the story

The children's response to the story now forms the basis of the rest of the session. It's important that they're encouraged to be spontaneous and really engage with the characters and the action. Here you will of course want to focus on the forms of response that are best suited to your situation, but the first one, 'Discussion', should never be missed out.

Discussion

Keep it lively, informal, chatty – and don't let any child feel silly or wrong, whatever they say or ask. The important thing is that they grow by being able to interact freely with the text. You may want to feed in some of their questions or reactions to the storytelling in the all-age worship. Most importantly, don't be anxious about this section – and don't let the discussion become either too long or too heavy! Just enjoy a bit of a chat with the children.

Song

Some songs are suggested. Either revisiting well-known ones or learning new ones can be fun, and perhaps sometimes the children can teach some of the new ones to the adults in the all-age worship. However, be careful not to let the Junior Church session degenerate into mere rehearsal. Let them have fun singing the songs, confident that even imperfectly sung they will still form acceptable worship. If some of the children have instruments, there's no reason why they couldn't be used at this time. All the songs recommended in these pages can be found in one or more of the following Kevin Mayhew publications (among others):

- *Kidsource*
- *The Source*
- *The Children's Hymn Book*
- *21st Century Folk Hymnal*

Art and craft

This will probably form quite a big part of the session: children of all ages and abilities can work together to produce models, drawings, paintings, etc. A few ideas are suggested, but they don't need to be limited. This was the area where we found children really showed their ingenuity and made immensely valuable contributions, producing and effecting ideas that would never have occurred to us!

Some of the art and craft work will feed into the all-age worship, and the items especially designed to do that are indicated with a tick. You may want to put less emphasis on this item if you're not planning on focusing on it in the service. What is important, in the 'ticked' activities, is that the children know *why* they are preparing these things – a few simple words of explanation will help them to relate it to the story they have heard and the point you were trying to make.

In terms of drawing and painting, the options are limited only by the size of the group and the children's imaginations! They could build up over the three weeks a complete 'strip cartoon' of the whole story, to be used in introducing the theme in all-age worship. The pictures could be on a continuous frieze, or on cardboard placards held on poles by the children, or separate pictures fixed around the walls before the service starts. Children could enter at different points as the story is told, holding their placard, or . . . well, you think of your own ideas – they'll probably be better than mine, anyway.

Drama

A dramatised version of the story is included. It can simply be used as a dramatised reading, with different children literally reading the parts, or it could be developed if your group has a flair for it into something much bigger. Adapt it freely to suit your group. If you need more parts, try splitting the narrator's part between several children, or add in one or two new characters. During the free discussion of the story things might emerge that it would be good to include in the dialogue. Feel free to photocopy these pages and make your own alterations if you wish. The drama can then either be used simply as a teaching aid or rehearsed and presented in the all-age worship. An added touch might be to use a domestic tape recorder to record it – then each child could take home a recording of a play with their own voice on it!

Worksheet

This is included for you to use as you see fit. You could have some of the children colour in the pictures and display them at the service, or you could let a group work through the sheet as part of the session; or it could simply be given to them as a take-home sheet to help them remember the session and/or to share with their families.

All-age worship

This is the culmination of the unit, but please don't allow preparation for it to dominate and spoil the sessions. It's not a performance, and no one will mind if what the children produce isn't beautifully polished – the main thing is that they should be seen to be enjoying it.

The services are designed to be truly 'all age', involving the whole congregation, and – most importantly – giving opportunities for interaction across the age groups. There are no 'children's talks', but rather all-age activities.

HOW TO GET THE BEST FROM THIS BOOK

This approach needs to be reflected in the overall balance of the service, so that it is one in which all people can participate rather than a children's service with the adults as indulgent spectators. Let's take a look at the various elements:

Songs

Naturally, there will be songs specifically chosen by the children, or at least with them in mind. But including some more 'adult' hymns not only shows respect to the older worshippers but also requires the children to sample a more varied diet and hopefully broaden their taste.

Welcome and statement of the theme

An example is given, but please feel free to use your own words and adapt it for your own circumstances. It's an important element in the service, for it introduces the chosen theme and sets it in the wider context. It is also a jolly good opportunity to point out some of the creative work the children have done, and have it suitably acknowledged by the congregation.

Prayers

Again, an opening prayer is offered, but it's not mandatory! Local worship leaders will probably want to do something more appropriate to the particular setting.

Word and action

The Bible story selected from one of the weeks 1-3 is not only read but reinforced with an all-age activity. The essential point is to make this at once meaningful and enjoyable. If people enjoy it, they're far more likely to enter into it. One important point, though: you know your own congregation best, and are in a position to ensure that people aren't treated insensitively. If you know that Mrs X doesn't like being in the limelight, then avoid drawing attention to her. Finally, watch the time. People will warm to the subject and be difficult to stop! You will also then be deluged with responses, many of them duplicated in different groups. Keep the discussion short and to the point, and move on. And don't forget to consider setting up the action group (see Introduction, page 7) – people need to know this isn't just a talking shop!

Offertory prayer

All we do and give is a free response to what God does for and gives to us. The offertory prayer is a good opportunity to highlight that point. This helps to avoid religion becoming 'works centred' rather than being a free, joyful response to God's grace.

Reading

Because you're using imaginatively rewritten stories, it's very important to read from a standard Bible in the service, and this point should never be overlooked. Children – and especially the older ones and the young people – need to hear the Bible read and come to appreciate it for themselves.

Talk

It's marked 'optional', but it's actually quite an important part of the service. As with the Bible, the traditional sermon is too valuable (when done well) to throw away. In a service of this nature, a short talk helps develop and maintain the skills of listening and reasoning. Keep it short, though, or it will have the opposite effect! On the other hand, if the service is running over time, this is an element that could *occasionally* be omitted.

Notices and family news

All too often, notices are regarded as an intrusion, and ways are often found to 'get them out of the way'. But surely, this is the life of the Church that is being shared here – and should it not be offered to God, along with the lives of his people? In the service order, I've suggested putting the notices directly before the Intercessions, so they can then feed into the prayers, thus integrating them more closely into the worship.

This is also a suitable time to do something else – the 'Family news'. People who have, for example, a birthday, or a wedding anniversary, or perhaps who are changing jobs, retiring or whatever, can share that with the congregation. A supply of cards can be kept in the church, with a suitably general message in them, to be handed out to people along with the good wishes and applause of the congregation. This is one slot we daren't leave out at Anstey, or we hear about it!

Intercessions

If Jesus was 'the man for others', it's hard to imagine worship that is genuinely Christian and doesn't include some sort of intercession for others. You will certainly want to include some of the children's own concerns that have emerged in the sessions in these prayers. You might also want to use some of the artwork to help the congregation focus on particular things. Whoever leads these, try to ensure that they are done thoughtfully, with a concern for the whole of God's creation, and not just Christians.

Closing prayer/benediction

Another element that should be kept short but meaningful! This is where the congregation are sent out into the world to live in some way the values and ideals they have expressed in their worship.

Now, go to it!

Most importantly of all – use the material imaginatively; make it work *for you*. It is your servant, not your director. What matters is that all involved enjoy the sessions, learn about valuing and being valued, build relationships with each other and with 'staff', and learn along the way.

That's how Jesus worked whenever he could. And it's not a bad example to follow!

Unit 1
The story of Joseph

Overview of the unit

Theme: Joseph – from spoilt brat to wise governor

We take three key events:

Week 1: Joseph is sold into slavery

> Joseph, very much the spoilt favourite son, finally pushes his brothers too far and they decide to get rid of him. They think it's all over, but the generously proportioned lady has not even begun her swan-song . . .

Week 2: Joseph is imprisoned

> Joseph's fortunes begin to improve when he becomes the trusted servant of Potiphar, but he suffers a serious setback when he is falsely accused and imprisoned. However, even there, God does not forget Joseph.

Week 3: Joseph becomes governor of Egypt

> When Pharaoh has nightmares, Joseph is the one who interprets them and consequently is made governor with the task of saving Egypt from the worst ravages of famine. He does the job so well that the surrounding people come to Egypt to buy the spare food, and Joseph is reunited with his family.

All-age worship

> Here, you may choose to focus on any one of the three subthemes, but place it in the context of the overall story and theme: God's saving power to bring something good out of disaster. So while the specific theme chosen will be emphasised in the choice of 'Word and action' material, some of the art and craft work the children have done in the other weeks will be used to decorate the church and set the context of the wider story.

Important note

- ✔ The ticked activities in Weeks 1-3 are intended as the link material for the 'Word and action' slot in the all-age worship. You will only need to do this in one of the three weeks – depending on which week's subtheme is going to be the main emphasis in the service.

Week 1: Joseph is sold into slavery

Thinking about it

What's the point?

Joseph's troubles were largely of his own making (although his indulgent father didn't make things any easier). Yet God did not abandon him – on the contrary, God turned the disasters into opportunities and Joseph became a major figure in God's work of salvation. So God does not take a 'You've made your bed, you can lie in it' approach, but always seeks to bring good out of trouble – even if it is our own fault! Sometimes, as in Joseph's case, it takes an awful long time to happen, but God can do it.

Doing it

Prayer

Loving God,
thank you for being such a great God,
and loving us so much.
Help us today to learn more of your love
and to show it to one another.
Amen.

From the known to the unknown

Set one of the children aside (be careful not to choose one who's already unpopular or lacking social confidence) and say that (just as a game) you're going to give that child special treatment – not for any good reason, but just because you have taken a liking to that particular child. Perhaps you can find a special hat or jacket to confer as a mark of status. S/he need not do any work unless s/he wants to, but will be allowed to report back to you if any other children aren't doing what they should. Now, how do they feel about that? Is it fair? Is it going to encourage resentment, and alienate the chosen child? Then again, how does the 'special' child feel? Embarrassed, perhaps, to be set up for unpopularity in that way? Well, of course this is only a game – but the story this week is about someone who really did get that treatment.

Tell the story: Genesis 37:1-35

(See page 21 for a dramatised version of this story)

Joseph the brat

Jacob's sons weren't happy – and the cause of it all was Joseph. Joseph was Jacob's second-youngest son, and it was pretty obvious Jacob loved him more than he did the others – and they didn't like it. Especially when Joseph seemed to be getting big ideas – very big ideas, indeed!

'I say, you fellows,' he said, one day. 'I had this amazing dream. Like, we were all out harvesting the corn, right? And we tied up all the corn into sheaves, right? And your sheaves – you'll love this bit – your sheaves – right? – well, they all bowed down to mine.'

'I think we'd better go and check on those sheep,' said Dan to his brothers. 'We'd find them better company.'

Everyone agreed, and in no time at all they'd all gone off to the fields.

'I say!' Joseph exclaimed. 'Was it something I said?'

Even out in the fields, though, the brothers couldn't get Joseph out of their mind.

'D'you know what happened yesterday?' said Dan, angrily. 'Joseph was supposed to be helping a few of us to look after the sheep – well, he only went sneaking back to Dad and told him we were being careless.'

'And were you?' asked Levi.

'That's not the point,' Gad answered, looking embarrassed. 'The point is, he's our brother and he goes sneaking off and telling tales. And it's not as if he ever does any work himself!'

'Well, he wouldn't, would he?' Judah interrupted. 'Not with that coat Dad's given him. Have you seen the length of those sleeves – how can he do a man's work with that on?'

'That's just it,' Levi added. 'Dad doesn't want his dear little favourite son doing nasty things like work, does he? *That's* why he gave him the coat in the first place.'

'He's just too big for his boots,' said Gad. 'Anyone would think he was a rock star – whatever one of those is.'

'Oh, look – here he comes,' said Dan. 'I bet he's come to spy on us again. Dad probably sent him. Look at him with his fancy coat and his delicate skin – a day's honest work would kill him. Come to think of it, why wait a day? – let's do it anyway.'

'Good idea!' Asher agreed. 'We can dump his body in one of these dried-up wells and tell Dad a wolf got him – see what happens to all his big ideas then!'

'I don't think we should do that,' said Reuben, quietly. 'Why not just dump him in the pit, but not kill him – that should teach him a lesson.'

Reuben thought he might be able to rescue Joseph later when the others had calmed down a bit – but that wasn't how it worked out.

Joseph got closer. 'I say, you fellows,' he began, 'I've had the most amazing dream . . . Hey! What? Get off me! Ow! You just wait until Dad finds out.'

The brothers had pounced. Off came the beautiful long-sleeved coat, and down Joseph went into the deep, dark well – luckily it had dried out. 'And keep quiet,' grunted Levi, 'or it'll be worse for you.'

Judah had an idea. 'Let's not kill the brat,' he said. 'Let's sell him as a slave. Look, there are some traders passing – I bet they'd give us a good price. After all, we shouldn't be *too* cruel – he *is* our brother.'

The others agreed, and they stopped the traders. 'Want to buy a slave?' asked Dan, craftily. 'He's a good, strong lad, and a really hard worker.'

The trader wasn't impressed. 'What – with smooth skin like that? Never done a day's work in his life, if you ask me. I'll give you a tenner for him.'

'You joke, of course,' Gad responded. 'He's worth thirty of anyone's money.'

'Don't make me laugh,' scoffed the trader, 'it's bad for my image. Let's say fifteen.'

'Twenty-five,' said Asher.

'Twenty,' said the trader, 'and that's my last offer.'

'Done!' said Judah. 'Now, we've got to make this convincing. Gad, you kill one of the goats and we'll rip up Joseph's coat and cover it in its blood – then we need to get our story straight before we see Dad.'

When they arrived home, they told Jacob the tale they'd agreed. 'It was horrible,' said Dan. 'A big vicious beastie with long claws and enormous teeth. We didn't stand a chance against it.'

'We tried, though,' Levi assured him. 'Didn't we, Asher?'

'Oh, yes, but it was too fierce. Here's Joseph's coat, though – we thought you'd like to have that back.'

Jacob looked at the horrible, bloodstained rag that had once been Joseph's coat. 'I'll never be happy again,' he moaned. 'I'll die a sad and lonely man, without my son.'

Now, I know Jacob was upset, but I don't suppose his other sons were very flattered by that. Anyway, you and I know that Joseph wasn't dead at all. In fact, he was only just beginning the adventures of his life! Oh dear – is that the time? I'll have to tell you about those another day.

Respond to the story

Discussion

Why did Joseph's brothers resent him?
- Because he didn't do any work?
- Because he thought he was better than them?
- Because he was Dad's favourite?

Is work the only thing that's important?
- What else is important?
- Do we need both work and rest/play in our lives?

Song

One or more of the following songs might be used here and/or in the all-age worship:

Jesus put this song into our hearts
Kum ba yah
Let love be real*
Nobody's a nobody
Shalom, my friends

* Use the version in *21st Century Folk Hymnal* (Kevin Mayhew)

Art and craft

✔ Take two large sheets of paper (e.g. flip-chart paper) and write the headings 'Being' on one and 'Doing' on the other. (See 'Word and action' in the All-age worship for how this would be used.) You might like to illustrate 'Being' with a drawing of a long-sleeved coat, and 'Doing' with a short-sleeved shirt or body warmer. Or, you could do what our group did: find some appropriate coats and let the children model them.

Draw or paint a picture of Joseph in his long-sleeved coat.

This is the key picture, but you might want to do others in addition to it, such as:

- Joseph down the well
- Joseph's brothers all conspiring against him
- Joseph being taken by camel into slavery

Drama

See the opposite page for a dramatised version of the story.

UNIT 1: WEEK 1

Drama: Joseph the brat

Narrator	Jacob's sons weren't happy – and the cause of it all was Joseph. Jacob loved him more than he did the others – and they didn't like it. Especially when Joseph seemed to be getting big ideas – very big ideas, indeed!
Joseph	I say, you fellows, I had this amazing dream. Like we were all out harvesting the corn, right? And we tied up all the corn into sheaves, right? And your sheaves – you'll love this bit – your sheaves – right? – well, they all bowed down to mine.
Dan	We'd better go and check the sheep – they'll be better company.
Narrator	Everyone agreed with Dan, and they all rushed off to the fields.
Joseph	I say! Was it something I said?
Narrator	Out in the fields, the brothers were still angry about Joseph.
Dan	D'you know what happened yesterday? Joseph was supposed to be helping Gad and me to look after the sheep – well, he only went sneaking back to Dad and told him we were being careless.
Gad	It's not as if he ever does any work – does he, Judah?
Judah	Well, he wouldn't, would he? Not with that coat Dad's given him. Have you seen the length of those sleeves – how can he do a man's work with that on?
Levi	That's just it. Dad doesn't want his dear little favourite son doing nasty things like work, does he? *That's* why he gave him the coat in the first place.
Gad	He's just too big for his boots. Anyone would think he was a rock star – whatever one of those is.
Dan	Oh, look – here he comes. Look at him with his fancy coat and his delicate skin – a day's honest work would kill him. Come to think of it, why wait a day – let's do it anyway.
Asher	Good idea! We can dump him in one of these dried-up wells and tell Dad a wolf got him – so much for his big ideas then!
Narrator	One of the brothers, Reuben, wanted to try and save Joseph.
Reuben	I don't think we should do that. Why not just dump him in the pit, but not kill him. That should teach him a lesson.
Narrator	By this time, Joseph had got closer.
Joseph	I say, you fellows, I've had the most amazing dream.
Narrator	He didn't get any further before the brothers pounced.
Joseph	Hey! What? Get off me! Ow! You just wait until Dad finds out.
Narrator	Off came the beautiful long-sleeved coat, and down Joseph went into the deep, dark well – luckily it had dried out. Then Judah had an idea.

Judah	Let's not kill the brat. Let's sell him as a slave. Look, there are some traders passing – I bet they'd give us a good price. After all, we shouldn't be *too* cruel – he *is* our brother.
Narrator	The others agreed, and they stopped the traders.
Dan	Want to buy a slave? Good, strong lad, and a really hard worker.
Trader	What – with smooth skin like that? Never done a day's work in his life, if you ask me. I'll give you a tenner for him.
Gad	You joke, of course. He's worth thirty of anyone's money.
Trader	Don't make me laugh, it's bad for my image. I'll give you twenty.
Judah	Done! Now, Gad, you kill one of the goats and we'll rip up Joseph's coat and cover it in its blood – then take it back to show Dad.
Narrator	When they arrived home, they told Jacob the tale they'd agreed.
Dan	It was horrible – a big vicious beastie with long claws and enormous teeth. We didn't stand a chance against it.
Narrator	Jacob looked at the horrible, bloodstained rag that had once been Joseph's coat.
Jacob	I'll never be happy again. I'll die sad and lonely, without my son.
Narrator	Now, I know Jacob was upset, but I don't suppose his eleven other sons were very flattered by that. Anyway, you and I know that Joseph wasn't dead at all. In fact, he was only just beginning the adventures of his life! Oh dear – is that the time? I'll have to tell you about those another day.

UNIT 1: WEEK 1

The Lord will not forsake his people. (Psalm 94:14)

WORDSEARCH

Find the following words in the grid:
COAT, LONG SLEEVES, JOSEPH, JACOB, FAVOURITE, DREAMER, WORK, PIT, SHEEP, BROTHERS, JEALOUS, GOAT, BLOOD, SOLD.

```
C S R E H T O R B O A T
S L E E T I R U O V A F
B R O T M E R S C O L D
B L O O D A D R A E M E
G E A L O U E X J O S J
O S E P H W O R K J E E
A R H R I T E D D A A A
T I P E J E A O L L L L
B H E N E D L O S O O O
L L S L E P U A C U U I
O L O N G S L E E V E S
O V J O S E P V O U R I
```

Join the dots to find the character in the story who came off worst.

23

Week 2: Joseph is imprisoned

Thinking about it

What's the point?

Things seem to be as bad as they can get, but even now God is at work. Joseph has obviously learned a lesson, and instead of alienating people he earns their trust. It's not a magic formula, but it does help God to work in the situation.

Doing it

Prayer

Loving God,
thank you for all our friends,
and especially for the people we meet here.
Help us to learn and grow together,
and to learn to trust each other and you.
Amen.

From the known to the unknown

Ask the children about people they trust – in general terms, mentioning no names. Why do they trust some people more than others? Perhaps there are some people they think are dishonest, others they think are just careless – and of course there are many they just don't know enough about: people they pass in the street, or see on buses, whom they wouldn't trust until they knew them. So trust is something we have to help grow – it doesn't just happen – and, as we'll see in this story, it makes it a lot easier for God to work when people trust one another.

Tell the story: Genesis 39-41

(See page 28 for a dramatised version of this story.)

Joseph the prisoner

Joseph had come a long way since his jealous brothers sold him as a slave. A very long way indeed – all the way to Egypt – but even there God was keeping a close eye on things. Joseph was bought by Potiphar – one of the top servants of the Pharaoh, or king, of Egypt. Potiphar liked Joseph. 'Why don't I put you in charge of all my house?' he said to him. 'You're obviously a good bloke, and I know I can trust you.'

Famous last words, you might say. Not that Joseph did anything wrong at all, mind you – someone (Potiphar's wife, no less) told some nasty lies about him, and guess where he ended up? In prison, that's where. 'Well,' he thought, 'this place is the pits! No, actually, I've been there, and nothing's *that* bad – but it's close.'

However, Joseph had obviously learned from past mistakes – learned to make people like him, not hate him – and it wasn't long before the prison guard got to trust him, just as Potiphar had. 'You'd better be in charge of the whole prison,' he said. 'And you can start by looking after these two rogues.' Joseph recognised two of the king's servants: Corky the wine waiter, and Bunny the Baker. No one had ever known their real names, and no one does to this day.

Joseph didn't ask what they'd done to get put in prison. 'Same as me, probably,' he thought. 'Nothing.' He helped them settle in, and they got on well enough. In fact, *they* began to like and trust Joseph, too. God was really working some miracles, wasn't he? – from being hated by his own brothers, Joseph was getting to be liked and trusted by everybody!

One morning, Corky and Bunny were looking sad enough to make a hyena cry! 'What's the matter?' asked Joseph.

'It's these dreams we've had,' Bunny answered. 'Weird – really weird.'

'Ah, well,' Joseph answered, 'dreams are God's business, and God and I are really close, you know? So why don't you tell me about them?' (A bit of the old Joseph showing there, I think, but we'll let it go.)

Corky told about his dream first. 'There was this vine, see – with three branches – and it sprouted buds, and then fruit, right in front of me. So I did what I'm best at – I picked the grapes, squeezed them into a cup and took them to Pharaoh. Just like that – I mean, it should have taken years for all that to happen!'

'That's easy,' Joseph told him. 'You've got just three days left in here – one for each branch – and then you'll have your old job back. So, how about you put a good word in for me when you get there?'

'Oh, sure, sure, of course – anything you say, Joseph.' But Corky's eyes were glazed over and he wasn't really listening any more – just imagining how he was going to spend his first week's pay.

Bunny thought this was really good – perhaps *his* dream meant something hopeful, too – so he told Joseph all about it.

'Well, it's like this: there I was, carrying three baskets of cakes on my head – best way, really, keeps your hands free for fly swatting – and the top basket had all Pharaoh's favourite food in it. You know, he's got a real thing about my lemon curd doughnuts with fondant icing. Anyway, before I could do anything about it, all these birds came and ate the food straight out of the top basket on my head. OK, so what does that mean, then?'

Joseph was sad. 'Not good, I'm afraid,' he said. 'You've got three days before you'll be out of here, as well – but you'll be too dead to enjoy it. And the birds are going to be pecking at your head. I mean, I'm sorry and all that, but don't blame me – I'm the messenger, not the manager.'

It all happened just the way Joseph had said. Three days later happened to be Pharaoh's birthday, so he decided to celebrate. Corky got his job back, and Bunny – well, you know what happened to poor Bunny.

Joseph waited, in prison, for Pharaoh to send for him, too. 'I know Corky will put a good word in for me,' he thought. 'Corky wouldn't forget.'

Corky forgot. Time went by, and still Joseph was in prison. 'Everyone's forgotten me,' he thought. 'I've lost my family, my dad thinks I'm dead, and now I'm just going to rot in this horrible prison and never see my brothers again.'

Well, Corky might have forgotten Joseph, but God hadn't. God knew exactly where Joseph was – and he had great plans for him. Joseph had changed a lot during the troubled times, and soon he was going to be just the person everybody wanted to know. But that's another story – for another time.

Respond to the story

Discussion

How do the children think Joseph felt when Potiphar's wife told lies about him?
- Angry?
- Afraid?
- Reluctant to trust or help anybody ever again?

Why was God able to work in this situation?
- Because Joseph trusted God?
- Because Joseph made it easy for people to trust him?

It would probably be worth reiterating here the earlier point about trust being something that has to grow – instantly trusting strangers is not trust but gullibility, and children in particular need to be very careful.

Song

One or more of the following songs might be used here and/or in the all-age worship:

He's got the whole world in his hand
Seek ye first the kingdom of God
This little light of mine
Whenever I'm afraid

Art and craft

✔ Go back to the discussion about the people whom the children trust. Keeping it light-hearted, think of people they should be able to trust: police, doctors, clergy, etc., and some they might be more reluctant to trust: politicians, strangers, tele-sales people. Now prepare some children to represent these in the all-age worship. You might make some simple badges – a red cross for the nurse, a 'Doctor on call' badge for the doctor, a rosette with 'Vote for me' on it for the politician. The tele-sales person could simply carry a telephone. (See 'Word and action' in the All-age worship for how all this would be used.)

Draw or paint a picture of Joseph in prison.

This is the key picture, but you might want to do others in addition to it, such as:
- Potiphar's wife
- the jailer
- the baker
- the wine waiter

Drama: Joseph the prisoner

Narrator	Joseph had come a long way since his jealous brothers sold him as a slave. A very long way indeed – all the way to Egypt – but even there God was keeping a close eye on things. Joseph was bought by Potiphar – one of the top servants of the Pharaoh, or king, of Egypt. Potiphar liked Joseph.
Potiphar	Why don't I put you in charge of all my house? You're obviously a good bloke, and I know I can trust you.
Narrator	Famous last words, you might say. Not that Joseph did anything wrong at all, mind you – someone (Potiphar's wife, no less) told some nasty lies about him, and guess where he ended up? In prison, that's where.
Joseph	Well, this place is the pits! No, actually, I've been there, and nothing's *that* bad – but it's close.
Narrator	Joseph had obviously learned from what his brothers did to him – learned to make people like him, not hate him – and it wasn't long before the prison guard got to trust him, just as Potiphar had.
Guard	You'd better be in charge of the whole prison. And you can start by looking after these two rogues.
Joseph	I recognise you. You're Corky, the king's personal wine waiter, and you're Bunny, his personal baker.
Narrator	No one had ever known their real names, and no one does to this day. Joseph helped them settle in, and soon *they* began to like and trust Joseph, too. God was really working some miracles, wasn't he? – from being hated by his own brothers, Joseph was getting to be liked and trusted by everybody! One morning, Corky and Bunny were looking sad enough to make a hyena cry!
Joseph	What's the matter with you, Bunny?
Bunny	It's these dreams we've had. Weird – really weird.
Joseph	Ah, well, dreams are God's business, and God and I are really close, you know? So why don't you tell me about them?
Narrator	A bit of the old Joseph showing there, I think, but we'll let it go.
Corky	There was this vine, see – with three branches – and it sprouted buds, and then fruit, right in front of me. So I picked the grapes, squeezed them into a cup and took them to Pharaoh. Just like that – I mean, all that should have taken years!
Joseph	That's easy, Corky. You've got just three days left in here – one for each branch – and then you'll have your old job back. So, how about you put a good word in for me when you get there?
Corky	[*Vaguely*] Oh, sure, sure, of course – anything you say, Joseph.
Narrator	Bunny thought this was really good – perhaps his dream meant something hopeful, too – so he told Joseph all about it.
Bunny	Well, it's like this: there I was, carrying three baskets of cakes on my head – best way, really, keeps your hands free for fly swatting

	– and the top basket had all Pharaoh's favourite food in it. You know, he's got a real thing about my lemon curd doughnuts with fondant icing. Anyway, before I could do anything about it, all these birds came and ate the food straight out of the top basket on my head. OK, so what does that mean, then?
Joseph	Not good, I'm afraid. In three days, you'll be out of here as well – but you'll be too dead to enjoy it. And the birds are going to be pecking at your head. I mean, I'm sorry and all that, but don't blame me – I'm the messenger, not the manager.
Narrator	Three days later happened to be Pharaoh's birthday, so he decided to celebrate. Corky got his job back, and Bunny – well, you know what happened to poor Bunny. Joseph waited, in prison, for Pharaoh to send for him, too.
Joseph	I know Corky will put a word in for me. Corky wouldn't forget.
Narrator	Corky forgot. Time went by, and still Joseph was in prison.
Joseph	Everyone's forgotten me. I've lost my family, my dad thinks I'm dead, and now I'm just going to rot in this horrible prison and never see my brothers again.
Narrator	Well, Corky might have forgotten Joseph, but God hadn't. God knew exactly where Joseph was – and he had great plans for him. Joseph had changed a lot during the troubled times, and soon he was going to be just the person everybody wanted to know. But that's another story – for another time.

THREE + ONE: FROM TROUBLE TO TRIUMPH

But the Lord was with Joseph and showed him steadfast love.
(Genesis 39-21)

Crack the code to complete the sentence. Even in bad times . . .

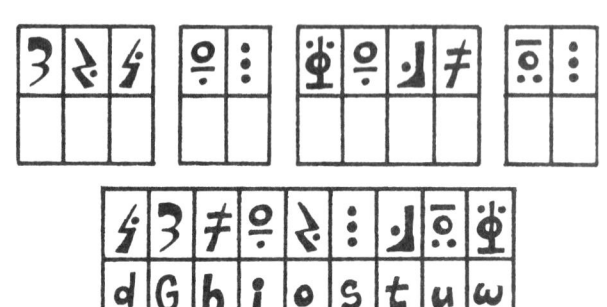

Key: d G h i o s t u w

WORDSEARCH
Find the following words in the grid:

GOD, REMEMBERS, JOSEPH, POTIPHAR, TRUST, LIES, WINE WAITER, BAKER, PRISON, DREAMS, THREE, DAYS, FAVOURITE, FOOD.

P	O	T	I	R	N	F	D	O	C	D	P
T	H	R	E	E	P	O	T	I	P	H	O
B	A	K	E	D	G	O	S	E	P	H	T
F	A	V	O	A	R	I	T	I	I	N	I
B	A	K	E	Y	A	I	T	E	R	O	P
F	O	D	A	S	Y	J	O	S	E	P	H
D	A	R	E	M	E	M	B	E	R	S	A
X	R	E	T	I	A	W	E	N	I	W	R
D	R	A	E	R	E	M	E	M	B	S	U
O	G	M	H	R	U	C	H	N	U	E	S
O	J	S	Q	W	E	S	R	T	Y	I	T
F	A	V	O	U	R	I	T	E	A	L	S

How many of the wine waiter's bottles can you find here?

30

Week 3: Joseph becomes governor of Egypt

Thinking about it

What's the point?

It hasn't been easy – no snap-of-the-fingers quick fix – but out of all the trouble God now brings a great result. However, while it isn't a quick fix, it isn't a case of 'just sit back and wait', either. A number of different people have played their part. So we need not only to trust God to bring good out of trouble, but also to be alert to how he might be hoping to use us in the process.

Doing it

Prayer

Loving God,
we know you are always with us,
in good times and in bad.
Please help us to learn together
and to grow in our friendship and trust
with you and with each other.
Amen.

From the known to the unknown

Take in a simple jigsaw – the kind with large pieces, designed for very young children, would be best. Hide one of the pieces in a pocket or handbag, and then distribute the remaining pieces among some of the children and ask them to put it together. When they get stuck, you can play them along for a few moments before triumphantly producing the remaining piece and making the jigsaw complete. You can then explain that sometimes God's purpose is like a jigsaw – a lot of pieces have to come together, and a lot of people have to play their part.

Tell the story: Genesis 41

(See page 35 for a dramatised version of this story.)

Joseph the governor

Pharaoh, the king of Egypt, was not happy. 'What do I pay all these magicians and mumbo-jumboers for,' he grumbled, 'if when I want just a little thing like to be told what my dreams mean, no one can do it?'

Corky, the palace wine waiter, suddenly remembered something important he'd forgotten to tell Pharaoh.*

'You remember that time when you put me in prison?' he said. 'Well, I met

---

* Can the children remember from last week what it was?

this Hebrew slave there – Joseph or Jonah or something,* he was called – anyway, when I had a strange dream, he told me what it meant. And he was right, too – *and* he interpreted Bunny the Baker's dream as well, but Bunny wasn't as lucky as me. Anyway, I just thought you might be interested. Now, I've got this nice drop of wine for you . . .'

'Never mind the wine,' said Pharaoh, impatiently. 'Get me this Joel character, or whatever his name is.'

So Joseph was sent for. 'What? Go and see Pharaoh? But I look awful – d'you know what time it is?'

'Never mind that,' the guard growled at him. 'You'll look a sight worse if you argue – now get along.'

So Pharaoh told Joseph all about his strange dream.

'In my dream I was standing by the river meditating – the way you do – when these seven big, fat cows came up out of the river. "Well," I thought, "they've been well fed." And even as I thought it, these seven other cows came up, as well – really thin and ugly. Then, while I was watching, what d'you think happened? The seven thin, ugly cows gobbled up the seven fat ones. Just like that – bones and all. That did it – I woke up. Well, you would, wouldn't you?'

'I think I can help with that,' Joseph began.

'You'll speak when you're spoken to,' Pharaoh interrupted. 'I haven't finished yet. I went back to sleep, and dreamed about these seven ears of corn – really good, ripe corn. If Bunny the baker had used corn like that I might have let him keep his job – and his head. But I digress. Then these seven other ears of corn sprang up – all thin and weak, and not the sort of thing you'd feed to your pet pooch. And guess what happened then?† The seven thin ears of corn swallowed the ripe ears all up. OK. That's it. Talk. And make it good – I hear you're spot on with this sort of thing. So what does it mean?'

'Well, it's not really me, Your Majesty,' Joseph answered. 'It's God who tells me what these things mean. Think of the cows and the ears of wheat as years. You've got seven good years coming, when the farming will do really well. But then you're going to have seven terrible years – and all the goodness of the first seven years will be completely swallowed up by the bad ones.'

Pharaoh was horrified. 'But what can we do?' he cried.

'What you need, Your Majesty,' Joseph told him, 'is a really good governor: someone really wise and clever – and who listens to what God says – who can manage the good years, and save as much food as possible to see you through the bad ones. Of course, where you find a guy like that's another matter.'

'Seems to me I'm looking at him,' Pharaoh said. 'Right, you're it. Whatever you say goes, from now on. No one in Egypt's greater than you – except me, of course. Well, what are you waiting for? Get managing.'

---

* Which was it?
† Can the children guess?

Joseph did a really good job. He had big storehouses built, and every bit of food that wasn't strictly needed was saved. Then, seven years later, when the bad years came – just as God had told him they would – there was food for all the people. And when the famine spread worldwide, people from other nations soon realised there was food in Egypt, and started coming to Joseph to buy some. And it wasn't long before Joseph's father Jacob heard about it. Of course, he didn't know it was Joseph who was the brains behind it – he thought Joseph was long dead – but he heard there was food there, and he called his sons to him.

'I want you to go to Egypt, and find this governor fellow, and buy some food. And don't come back here without it.'

So, of course, you can guess what happened*. To cut a very long story short, Jacob was overjoyed to find that Joseph was alive after all – and not only alive but a very important person in Egypt – and the whole family went to live with him there. 'Trust God,' Jacob said, 'to bring something good out of all that trouble!'

Respond to the story

Discussion

How do the children think Corky felt when he realised he'd forgotten about Joseph?

- Embarrassed?
- Sorry?

Over the past three weeks, you've put together a kind of jigsaw story. Can the children remember what the different 'pieces' were?

- Joseph started out as someone who wasn't really very nice to know
- He had to learn his lesson from what happened when he upset his brothers
- Potiphar came to trust Joseph
- After a setback, Joseph had to earn the trust of his jailer
- Joseph interpreted Corky's dream
- Corky forgot about the last piece in the puzzle, and had to have his memory jogged by Pharaoh

But none of this would have helped if Joseph had not been open to God.

Song

One or more of the following songs might be used here and/or in the all-age worship:

God cares for all creation
God has a perfect plan for me
Let us sing your glory, Lord
Lord, the light of your love is shining
Safe in the Father's hands
So I'll trust

* Can they?

Art and craft

✔ Ask the children to think about a modern-day situation where someone is in trouble and needs to be rescued. (See 'Word and action' in the All-age worship for how this would be used.) What different characters would need to be involved in the rescue? For example (and this is just a suggestion), in the case of a mountain rescue the police might be alerted first, and then call in the mountain rescue team, who might use a tracker dog to locate the victim in the snow. They'd need a trained first-aider or perhaps a paramedic on hand to give the necessary on-the-spot treatment, and possibly a helicopter pilot and helicopter winchman to airlift the person to hospital where a team of doctors and nurses would take over. Of course, you could go on and on, but try to keep the children focused on just the basic team for now. The point is that when God brings good out of disaster he usually has to put quite a complex jigsaw together to make it happen – as was the case for Joseph. And sometimes we can be part of that jigsaw.

✔ Divide a piece of paper into roughly equal sections and write one of the characters in each. Then, between now and the all-age worship you can photocopy and guillotine this, keeping one copy intact, so as to end up with a number of sets of cards (how many you need will depend on the size of your congregation). The intact copy can be photocopied onto an overhead projector acetate, or you can simply make a list in large writing on a flip-chart or board.

Draw or paint a picture of Joseph being reunited with his father, Jacob.

This is the key picture, but you might want to do others in addition to it, such as:

- Joseph in front of Pharaoh
- Joseph in his official governor's robes
- Pharaoh telling Joseph his dream

Drama

See the opposite page for a dramatised version of the story.

Drama: Joseph the governor

Pharaoh What's the point of being Pharaoh, if when I want just a little thing like to be told what my dreams mean, no one can do it?

Narrator Corky, the palace wine waiter, suddenly remembered something important he'd forgotten to tell Pharaoh.

Corky Er, Your Majesty, you remember that time when you put me in prison? Well, I met this Hebrew slave there – Joseph or Jonah or something, he was called – anyway, when I had a strange dream, he told me what it meant. And he was right, too – *and* he interpreted Bunny the Baker's dream as well, but Bunny wasn't as lucky as me. Anyway, I just thought you might be interested.

Pharaoh Get me this Joel character, or whatever his name is.

Narrator So Joseph was sent for.

Joseph What? Go and see Pharaoh? But I look awful – d'you know what time it is?

Guard Never mind that. You'll look a sight worse if you argue – now get along.

Narrator So Pharaoh told Joseph all about his strange dream.

Pharaoh I was standing by the river meditating – the way you do – when these seven fat cows came up out of the river. 'Well,' I thought, 'they've been well fed.' And just then, these seven other cows came up, as well – really thin and ugly. And while I was watching, what d'you think happened? The seven thin, ugly cows gobbled up the seven fat ones. Just like that – bones and all. Well, that did it – I woke up. Well, you would, wouldn't you?

Joseph I think I can help with that.

Pharaoh You'll speak when you're told to – I haven't finished yet. I went back to sleep, and dreamed about these seven ears of corn – really good, ripe corn. If Bunny the baker had used corn like that I might have let him keep his job – and his head. But I digress. Then these seven other ears of corn sprang up – all thin and weak, and not the sort of thing you'd feed to your pet pooch. And guess what happened then? The seven thin ears of corn swallowed the ripe ears all up. OK. That's it. Talk. And make it good – I hear you're spot on with this sort of thing. So what does it mean?

Joseph Well, it's not really me, Your Majesty. It's God who tells me what these things mean. Think of the cows and the wheat as years. You'll have seven good years, when the farming will do really well, and then seven terrible years – and all the goodness of the first seven years will be completely swallowed up by the bad ones.

Pharaoh   [*Horrified*] But what can we do?

Joseph   What you need, Your Majesty, is a really good governor: someone really wise and clever – and who listens to what God says – who can manage the good years, and save as much food as possible to see you through the bad ones. Of course, where you find a guy like that's another matter.

Pharaoh   Seems to me I'm looking at him. Right, whatever you say goes, from now on. No one in Egypt's greater than you – except me, of course. Well, what are you waiting for? Get managing.

Narrator   Joseph had big storehouses built, and every bit of food that wasn't strictly needed was saved. Then, seven years later, when the bad years came – just as God had told him they would – there was food for all the people. And when the famine spread worldwide, people from other nations soon realised there was food in Egypt, and started coming to Joseph to buy some. And it wasn't long before Joseph's father Jacob heard about it. Of course, he didn't know it was Joseph who was the brains behind it – he thought Joseph was long dead – but he heard there was food there, and he called his sons to him.

Jacob   I want you to go to Egypt, and find this governor fellow, and buy some food. And don't come back here without it.

Narrator   So of course, you can guess what happened. To cut a very long story short, Jacob was overjoyed to find that Joseph was alive after all – and not only alive but a very important person in Egypt – and the whole family went to live with him there.

Jacob   Trust God to bring something good out of all that trouble!

UNIT 1: WEEK 3

A man who has God's spirit in him. (Genesis 41:38)

These pictures look the same but can you spot 10 differences?

WORDSEARCH

Find the following words in the grid: GOD, PHARAOH, JOSEPH, DREAMS, FAMINE, SEVEN, WHEAT, COWS, SAVE, BARNS, GOVERNOR, SWALLOWED.

G	O	V	E	R	N	G	O	D	C	O	W
A	B	D	R	E	A	N	S	A	V	C	H
M	A	M	I	N	V	L	J	O	S	O	A
I	R	P	H	A	R	A	O	H	C	W	R
N	N	O	V	E	R	N	S	E	P	S	A
E	S	A	V	S	M	A	E	R	D	B	O
W	A	L	L	O	W	N	P	H	A	R	H
P	H	A	R	A	I	O	H	E	V	E	N
D	R	E	E	M	A	L	L	O	W	E	E
R	S	W	A	L	L	O	W	E	D	N	V
E	N	F	G	T	O	V	E	R	N	O	E
A	T	R	O	N	R	E	V	O	G	R	S

Week 4: All-age worship

Opening Song

A song praising and celebrating the faithfulness of God

Welcome and statement of the theme

Get one or more of the children to point out or hold up the pictures as you sum up the story:

In Junior Church during the past few weeks, we've been following the story of Joseph – the one in the Old Testament, with the special coat, not the other one! We saw how he started off as a bit of a spoilt brat, to be honest, with his long-sleeved coat that wasn't designed for working in, and how his dreaming and big ideas made his brothers so mad that they sold him into slavery and told their father he'd been killed by a wild animal.

Then we followed him to Egypt, where he became a slave to Potiphar, a servant of the king, and actually won Potiphar's trust – but, just as he was doing well, Potiphar's wife told lies about him and poor old Joseph ended up in prison. Even there, though, he soon earned the trust of the jailer who put him in charge of the other prisoners. While he was there, God used him to interpret some other prisoners' dreams, and that made a big impression. So, when Pharaoh had strange dreams, Joseph was sent for to tell Pharaoh what they meant. Joseph foretold a great famine, and Pharaoh was so impressed he made him governor of Egypt.

It ended up with the whole world coming to him for help when the famine spread, and that was how eventually a much wiser and nicer Joseph was reunited with his father and brothers.

Well, that in a rather generous nutshell is the general picture, but today we're going to concentrate on: [*Name the episode of your choice*]

Prayer

– use whichever is appropriate

Based on Week 1

Loving God,
we thank you for giving us an important place
in your purpose for the world,
and for sharing your hopes and dreams
and visions with us.
Please forgive us for the times we find it difficult
to get on well with one another,
or with our neighbours,
and help us to remember
that everybody is important to you.
Through Jesus Christ our Lord.
Amen.

Based on Week 2

Loving God,
we thank you for being with us
even in the bad times of life,
and for helping us to learn from our own mistakes.
Please forgive us for the times
when we haven't trusted you enough,
and help us to grow in our faith.
Through Jesus Christ our Lord.
Amen.

Based on Week 3

Thank you, loving God,
for caring so much for each of us.
Thank you for the people you put us with,
and the opportunities you give us
to serve you in often unexpected ways.
Please forgive us for the times
when we forget about your blessings
or each other's needs,
and help us to live together as your people,
open to the special gifts each one of us has.
Through Jesus Christ our Lord.
Amen.

Word and action

– use whichever is appropriate

From Week 1

Have the story read in either narrative or dramatised form. Point out to the congregation the significance of the long-sleeved coat – Joseph wasn't expected to do his share of the work. We could (very broadly) summarise Joseph and his brothers by saying that he was all 'being' and they were all 'doing'. What about this church? Have we got the balance right? 'Brainstorm' the life of the church, and, as people mention things that go on, write them up as appropriate on one or other of the lists – church cleaning under 'Doing', prayer under 'Being', etc. If someone objects that it isn't that simple, recognise and emphasise that point but say that the rough-and-ready division will serve the purpose for now.

It's highly likely that the balance will be heavily tilted on the 'doing' side – running or attending meetings, fund-raising, administration, book-keeping. Even the 'being' things like prayer and worship inevitably involve some 'doing' as well (here you can acknowledge whoever raised this point earlier, if it was raised) – and that of course is right, but are we in danger of modelling to the world outside a gospel of salvation by works? Out of this service could come a review of the church's life, leading perhaps to some specific initiatives to give busy people more 'space' and create a more relaxed atmosphere – as long as that 'review' doesn't itself become just one more burden for the committed people to carry!

From Week 2

Have the story read in either narrative or dramatised form. Point out that the basis of the whole story is trust – sometimes trust rewarded, sometimes betrayed. Get the children to come to the front with their badges/props, and introduce them briefly. Ask the congregation to decide which ones they would trust and which they would treat with caution. Of course, there may be some politicians or tele-sales people in the congregation – and, even if not, you will need to make the point about not prejudging people. There's a general tendency to distrust people in occupations such as that, but there are good, honest people among them – just as there are (fortunately very few) dishonest or careless doctors and nurses.

Ultimately, we all need to trust each other if society is going to work well, but *real* trust only comes when we get to know people and, hopefully, as they get to know us.

From Week 3

Have the cards randomly given out as people arrive at the church. At this point in the service, divide the congregation into groups and ask them to imagine the same situation you presented to the children. They are to assemble a team from the cards they have, and the personnel the children have identified are listed on the overhead or board. Undoubtedly, no group will start out with the right combination of cards, and they will need to swap around the church (encourage them to move around freely) in order to assemble their team. There will also be some cards left over, but to save time stress that each group need only assemble one team. If you like, you could speed things up by making it a competition and stopping when the first team is formed.

You can now simply point out that in order for this single mission to be accomplished, a kind of jigsaw puzzle of skills and resources had to be completed. God worked a bit like that in the story of Joseph, and we're now going to hear the final part of that story in which the pieces eventually came together. (The context was set at the beginning of the service but if you want to recap that now, feel free to do so.)

Song 2

Offering

This may be introduced as our offering of ourselves and our resources for God to use in his redemptive work.

Offertory prayer

Loving God,
we thank you for your gift of grace,
able to bring good out of any difficulties.
We offer you our small gifts,

that people now experiencing dark and difficult times
may know the promise of your love.
Amen.

Song 3

Reading

Romans 8:35-end read from a standard Bible. Introduce it with words such as: Paul declares his faith that nothing – absolutely nothing – can ever separate us from God's love; something that Joseph would certainly have agreed with.

Talk (optional)

It's rather important to say here that this kind of faith does not mean we belittle people's problems or question the faith of people who despair. Rather it means that our faith gives us genuine hope which allows us to share their troubles without resorting to easy clichés.

Notices and family news

Prayers of intercession

These could be led entirely by the minister or other adult(s), and/or could include some prayers written by the children themselves – or simply some points that they have raised in discussion.

Song 4

Closing prayer/benediction

Unit 2
Israel in Babylon: from military defeat to moral victory

Overview of the unit

Theme: God brings victory out of defeat

We take three key events:

Week 1: Shadrach, Meshach and Abednego

King Nebuchadnezzar of Babylon gets above himself and tells everyone to worship his statue, but three Jewish slaves refuse – even under the threat of being burned alive.

Week 2: The king learns that pride goes before a fall

Daniel warns King Nebuchadnezzar that his arrogance will cost him dearly – but there's no teacher like experience. Nebuchadnezzar is brought to the depths of existence, where he eventually recognises God as the true power in the universe.

Week 3: Daniel in the lions' den

Daniel sticks to his principles and refuses to stop praying, even though the penalty is to be turned into lion fodder. When he survives that, the king is so impressed he does the unthinkable and changes the hitherto unchangeable 'law of the Medes and Persians', i.e. 'We've always done things this way'.

All-age worship

Here, you may choose to focus on any one of the three subthemes, but place it in the context of the overall story and theme: God's redemptive power. So while the specific theme chosen will be emphasised in the choice of 'Word and action' material, some of the art and craft work the children have done in the other weeks will be used to decorate the church and set the context of the wider story.

Important note

✔ The ticked activities in Weeks 1-3 are intended as the link material for the 'Word and action' slot in the all-age worship. You will only need to do this in one of the three weeks – depending on which week's subtheme is going to be the main emphasis in the service.

Week 1: Shadrach, Meshach and Abednego

Thinking about it

What's the point?

Babylon might have had all the military power, but that doesn't have the final word. Ultimately, ideas and beliefs are stronger than weapons, and the moral victory is still there to be fought for and won.

Doing it

Prayer

Loving God,
thank you for giving us time
to be with each other and you.
Help us to enjoy the time we have,
and to grow in our faith and commitment to you.
Amen.

From the known to the unknown

What's the price of being one of the 'in' set? The right kind of trainers? The latest model of bike? Sympathise with the children – these things feel important at that age. (When they're older they'll learn differently – then it'll be cars and credit ratings!) How much easier it is to worship idols than to stand apart from the crowd!

Tell the story: Daniel 3

(See page 49 for a dramatised version of this story.)

God's resistance

This is the story of Shadrach, Meshach and Abednego.*

It was a hot day in Babylon – every day was a hot day in Babylon, but this one was about to get hotter because King Nebuchadnezzar had had one of his silly ideas. 'Everyone must worship this statue of me,' said King Nebuchadnezzar, 'because it's beautiful – well, it would be, wouldn't it? And anyone who doesn't want to worship this statue of me will be burned in the burning fiery furnace – so there!'

The statue was over 25 metres high, and made of solid gold. 'And I'm worth every ounce of it,' said Nebuchadnezzar, 'because I'm the bestest

---

* Actually, the names are quite rhythmic, aren't they? Would the children enjoy saying them a few times? A fun way of telling the story would be to get the children to join in with them. Every time you say all three names together, ask, 'Who?' and let the children repeat them.

king what ever was, and I write poems, like, you know.' Then he started chanting. 'Worship me, worship me, or I'll burn you horribly. When you hear the trumpets blowing, bow your heads and let's get going. When you hear the drummers bashing, hit the deck and say I'm smashing.'

In the crowd were Shadrach, Meshach and Abednego. They were Jewish men, captured by King Nebuchadnezzar when he conquered Jerusalem – and they weren't impressed. 'It's enough to make you *cringe*,' said Shadrach, 'but I'm certainly not going to *bow* – not to that great big pile of rubbish, and not to his statue, either.'

King Nebuchadnezzar was just getting into his stride. 'Come and praise me, everybody; I'm your king and I'm your god-ee.'

Even Nebuchadnezzar looked a bit embarrassed by that one. The bandmaster decided someone had to do something about it, and started the music. Everybody bowed down. Everybody except Shadrach, Meshach and Abednego.

'I'm standing up for the one true God,' said Shadrach.

'Me too,' added Meshach.

'Me five,' said Abednego.

'Really, Abednego!' exclaimed Meshach. 'When are you going to learn to count!'

'A bit late for that, I think,' Abednego answered. 'The king doesn't look too pleased.'

Nebuchadnezzar was dancing up and down with rage. And his dancing was even worse than his poetry. 'Bow down!' he screamed at them. 'Bow down and worship my statue.'

'Well, thank goodness he's stopped doing silly rhymes, anyway,' said Abednego.

The king went on. 'If you don't bow, I'm going to burn you. You need a lesson and I'm going to learn you.'

The burning fiery furnace seemed almost a relief after that. The soldiers opened the door and pushed Shadrach, Meshach and Abednego in. Hot? You've never felt anything like it – and they hadn't got a factor 35 between them.

Outside the furnace, the king was still carrying on. 'Everybody, sing my praises, or like them you'll go to blazes!'

Before he could get even worse he stopped and looked through the furnace window, and couldn't believe his eyes.

'I say,' he said to his chief adviser, 'didn't we put *three* men into the fire to burn?'

'Yes, Your Majesty, I counted them all in.'

King Nebuchadnezzar looked worried. 'Then why are there four of them in there now, and why are they walking about, and why does one of them look like some kind of a god? Oh, my . . . word! Get them out! Get them out!'

The door was opened, and out came Shadrach, Meshach and Abednego, and there wasn't a singed hair between them.

Nebuchadnezzar decided it was time to get sensible. 'No more golden statues from now on,' he said. 'From now on we worship the God of Shadrach, Meshach and Abednego.'

And everyone agreed. And they were all very pleased. Especially Shadrach, Meshach and Abednego.

Respond to the story

Discussion

How do the children think Shadrach, Meshach and Abednego felt when told they had to worship the statue?

- Amused?
- Embarrassed?
- Angry?

How did they feel when they realised they were going to be burned to death?

- Terrified?
- Tempted to go along with it?
- Angry with God for getting them into this mess?

It's probably worth pointing out here that fire *is* dangerous, and just because we're Christians, that doesn't mean we can play with it and not get burned!

Song

One or more of the following songs might be used here and/or in the all-age worship:

Father, I place into your hands
How great is our God
Hey, now, everybody sing
I'm gonna click, click, click
Lift his name high
Sing and shout your praise to our God

Art and craft

✔ Have some magazines/catalogues handy, and pick up the earlier discussion. Get the children to cut out what they see as important social accessories or identifiers, and make a display of these by sticking them on to a large board or sheet of paper. Then write the following texts in large print on two separate pieces of A4 paper: 'Choose this day whom you will serve', and 'We will serve the Lord'. (It's a cut-down version of Joshua 24:15.) Finally, photocopy each sheet on to a different colour card, and cut it up so that each word is on a separate card. You will need enough copies for each worshipper to be given one word of each colour. See 'Word and action' in the All-age worship for how this would be used.

Draw or paint a picture of Shadrach, Meshach and Abednego walking nonchalantly in the furnace.

This is the key picture, but you might want to do others in addition to it, such as:

- the golden statue
- King Nebuchadnezzar looking proud
- King Nebuchadnezzar getting angry
- the people bowing down to worship, but three standing upright

Drama

See the opposite page for a dramatised version of the story.

Drama: God's resistance

Narrator	It was a hot day in Babylon – every day was a hot day in Babylon, but this one was about to get hotter because King Nebuchadnezzar had had one of his silly ideas.
Nebuchadnezzar	Everyone must worship this statue of me because it's beautiful – well, it would be, wouldn't it? And anyone who doesn't want to worship this statue of me will be burned in the burning fiery furnace – so there!
Narrator	The statue was over 25 metres high, and made of solid gold.
Nebuchadnezzar	And I'm worth every ounce of it, because I'm the bestest king what ever was, and I write poems, like, you know. [*Chants*] Worship me, worship me, or I'll burn you horribly. When you hear the trumpets blowing, bow your heads and let's get going. When you hear the drummers bashing, hit the deck and say I'm smashing.
Narrator	In the crowd were Shadrach, Meshach and Abednego. They were Jewish men, captured by King Nebuchadnezzar when he conquered Jerusalem – and they weren't impressed.
Shadrach	It's enough to make you *cringe*, but I'm certainly not going to *bow* – not to that great big pile of rubbish, and not to his statue, either.
Narrator	King Nebuchadnezzar was just getting into his stride.
Nebuchadnezzar	Come and praise me, everybody; I'm your king and I'm your god-ee.
Narrator	Even Nebuchadnezzar looked a bit embarrassed by that one. The bandmaster decided someone had to do something about it, and started the music. Everybody bowed down. Everybody except Shadrach, Meshach and Abednego.
Shadrach	I'm standing up for the one true God.
Meshach	Me too.
Abednego	Me five.
Meshach	Really, Abednego! When are you going to learn to count!
Abednego	A bit late for that, I think. The king doesn't look too pleased.
Narrator	Nebuchadnezzar was dancing up and down with rage. And his dancing was even worse than his poetry.
Nebuchadnezzar	Bow down! Bow down and worship my statue.
Abednego	Well, thank goodness he's stopped doing silly rhymes, anyway.

Nebuchadnezzar	If you don't bow, I'm going to burn you. You need a lesson and I'm going to learn you.
Narrator	Well, the burning fiery furnace seemed almost a relief after that. The soldiers opened the door and pushed Shadrach, Meshach and Abednego in. Hot? You've never felt anything like it – and they hadn't got a factor 35 between them. Outside the furnace, the king was still carrying on.
Nebuchadnezzar	Everybody, sing my praises, or like them you'll go to blazes!
Narrator	Before he got get even worse he stopped and looked through the furnace window, and couldn't believe his eyes. He called his chief adviser.
Nebuchadnezzar	I say, didn't we put *three* men into the fire to burn?
Adviser	Yes, Your Majesty, I counted them all in.
Nebuchadnezzar	Then why are there four of them in there now, and why are they walking about, and why does one of them look like some kind of a god? Oh, my . . . word! Get them out! Get them out!
Narrator	The door was opened, and out came Shadrach, Meshach and Abednego, and there wasn't a singed hair between them. Nebuchadnezzar decided it was time to get sensible.
Nebuchadnezzar	No more golden statues from now on. From now on we worship the God of Shadrach, Meshach and Abednego.
Narrator	And everyone agreed. And they were all very pleased. Especially Shadrach, Meshach and Abednego.

UNIT 2: WEEK 1

You shall have no other gods before me. (Exodus 20:3)

WORDSEARCH

Find the following words in the grid:
NEBUCHADNEZZAR, SHADRACH, MESHACH, ABEDNEGO, WORSHIP, MUSIC, IDOL, FURNACE, GOLD, BABYLON, JERUSALEM, GOD, KING, BURNING, UNHARMED.

```
S H A D R A P F U R N A T E
N O L Y B A B U A B J D N E
G O H M U S I R B U E J W W
G A B E D N H N Y R R E O B
O X M U S I C A L N U R R U
L S H A D R A C H I S U S R
F K I N S P H E K H A S H N
G N I R U B S B I G L A I I
L E D N E G E P N O E L V N
G O L N G I M U Y S M E S G
B C D C D E M R A H N U V A
E F A I N E B U C H A D N E
J Y D O G E N D E B A G O D
N E B U C H A D N E Z Z A R
```

Colour the dotted shapes black, and the other shapes yellow, red and orange, to set the fire ablaze!

Week 2: The king learns that pride goes before a fall

Thinking about it

What's the point?

There's nothing wrong with taking a healthy pride in our achievements, but sometimes it gets completely out of proportion. We need to recognise that while the use we make of our talents is down to us, the talents themselves come from God. That should help us to keep things in a healthy perspective.

Doing it

Prayer

Loving God,
thank you for all we are going to share this morning.
Help us always to remember
that all good things come from you
and to celebrate your love in the things we do together.
Amen.

From the known to the unknown

Have the children ever been over-confident, and had a salutary experience? Don't embarrass them by asking them to relate it, but it might be good to tell them one of yours – we've all had them – and enjoy the joke with them. A teacher or leader who can laugh at him or herself is a great example of maturity and confidence for children. You might even become a role model!

Tell the story: Daniel 4

(See page 56 for a dramatised version of this story.)

Nebuchadnezzar's bad hair day

King Nebuchadnezzar woke up in a terrible sweat. He'd had a really strange dream, and he wanted to know what it meant. 'Call the magicians!' he shouted. 'Send for the soothsayers! Find the fortune tellers! Oh, and just in case it's all in my mind, get me some psychotherapy. What d'you mean, it hasn't been invented yet!'

Everyone jumped to it, and before you could say, 'Superstitious old twit', he'd got all the dreamers, dabblers and diviners around him scratching their heads and trying to look as though they knew what they were talking about. They didn't. Then Daniel came in. Daniel had come to Babylon as a prisoner, captured when King Nebuchadnezzar conquered Jerusalem – but King Nebuchadnezzar had come to trust him because he knew God was with him. 'Thank heaven you've come,' said the king. 'Let me tell you my dream. There was a tree. Right? And it grew really big – I mean, dead impressive, you know – so big that it could be seen from anywhere on earth. Right? And it was good – covered in rich green leaves, with delicious fruit on it. And it gave shelter to the animals, and nesting space to all the birds – I mean it was a really great tree.'

'Sounds like it,' Daniel agreed. 'Go on.'

'There was an angel, right?' Nebuchadnezzar went on. 'A great, big, shiny angel, complete with harp, halo and heavenly hairdo – and he came down to the tree and started giving orders. "Chop down the tree!" he said. "Chop off its branches, right? Strip off its leaves, right? And scatter all the animals and birds." Well, I didn't know what was going on, but I knew it wasn't good.'

Daniel interrupted gently. 'What happened next?'

'Well,' Nebuchadnezzar continued, 'he told them to leave the stump in the ground – right? And he had a metal band put round it to stop it rotting, right? And then he got really weird. Started talking about the tree as if it were a person. "Let him be all wet with dew," he said. "And let him live with the animals," he said. "And let him lose his marbles completely, and be like an animal himself," he said. Right? And then he said something about everyone knowing that someone called the Most High is the one who's in charge around here. I tell you, it was scary. Right?'

'If he says "right" once more,' thought Daniel, 'I'll go mad – right? Oh, no!' Then he spoke to the king. 'You know, I wish this dream was about one of your enemies, Your Majesty, because I really like and respect you. But it's not. It's about you – you're the tree. Seems to me, God thinks you've forgotten who *is* the Most High around here, and you might need taking down a peg or two. Sorry about that, but you're going to have a really hard time. Of course, it might help if you started thinking about others instead of your own glory for a bit.'

Now, it may seem strange, but after all that worry and fretting, Nebuchadnezzar didn't take Daniel's advice – which was a pity. A year later, he was up on the roof, looking out at the city. 'Haven't I done well,' he said to himself. 'Other kings do stupid things like going to war, right? I've built cities – lots of them, with big buildings and tall towers, and all that stuff – right? I'm the greatest! the tops! I'm the Most High!'

He'd hardly said it before he heard a loud voice: 'You arrogant pipsqueak! Who d'you think gave you that power in the first place? *I* gave it, and *I'm* taking it away. Learn, Nebuchadnezzar – *learn*!'

Next thing he knew, he'd changed completely – his hair was all long and tangled and his neatly clipped finger-nails grew like claws. 'I can't be seen like this,' he thought. 'Better get away, right?' And that was the last thing he did think for a while, because he forgot how to. He lived like an animal, eating grass, always damp and smelly – even the skunks kept a safe distance from him. Now, if Nebuchadnezzar had had his wits about him, he'd have known what to do, but he didn't – he'd started to think like an animal, as well as look like one. So it took a long time for the point to sink in. When it did, it was as if someone had turned the light on. 'This is barmy!' thought Nebuchadnezzar. 'This is what comes of getting big ideas, and forgetting who it is that's really in charge around here. OK, God – look, I'm sorry, right? I mean, you're the Greatest – right? The Most High – right? I mean, you're just always going to be at the top – right?'

At that, King Nebuchadnezzar was transformed again – back to being human, back to the palace, back to things the way they were. Well, almost – there was one important difference.

Nebuchadnezzar did an amazing thing. He told his entire story to all his people – every gruesome little detail of it. 'I'm telling you this, right,' he said, 'so that you can all know who's really in charge around here, right? It's God, right? And he's the big boss, and he's the one we ought to praise – right?'

'Right!' said all the people. And they were.

Respond to the story

Discussion

Why do the children think Nebuchadnezzar ignored Daniel's advice to change his ways?

- Because he didn't take the dream seriously?
- Because he was too conceited to hear the warning?

Do they think Nebuchadnezzar was a really bad or silly man, or was he a good and actually very intelligent man, who just got above himself?

- What does that mean for us?

Song

One or more of the following songs might be used here and/or in the all-age worship:

God is good, we sing and shout it
How great is our God
I'm gonna click, click, click
Lord, the light of your love is shining
Praise God in his holy place
So if you think you are standing firm

Art and craft

✔ Prepare a monument to science. This could be as simple or as elaborate as you care to make it. You could use cardboard boxes to make a big pillar, and paint them like stone, or at the other extreme simply use a flip-chart page. At the top write the heading 'Science Rocks!' (See 'Word and action' in the All-age worship for how this would be used.) If you use the flip-chart method, you might want to make it look like a monument by drawing an outline with the heading done in the style of an inscription – but make sure you leave plenty of space to write during the service. Prepare a second inscription – 'God is love' – on a piece of card, large enough to cover the first.

Draw or paint a picture of a scruffy Nebuchadnezzar living with the animals.

This is the key picture, but you might want to do others in addition to it, such as:

- Nebuchadnezzar talking to Daniel
- the great tree
- the tree stump with its metal band

Drama: Nebuchadnezzar's bad hair day

Narrator	King Nebuchadnezzar woke up in a terrible sweat. He'd had a really strange dream, and he wanted to know what it meant.
Nebuchadnezzar	Call the magicians! Send for the soothsayers! Find the fortune tellers! And just in case it's all in my mind, get me some psychotherapy. What d'you mean, it hasn't been invented yet!
Narrator	Before you could say. 'Superstitious old twit', he'd got all the dreamers, dabblers and diviners around him scratching their heads and getting nowhere. Then Daniel came in.
Nebuchadnezzar	Thank heaven you've come! Let me tell you my dream. There was a tree. Right? And it grew really big – so big that it could be seen from anywhere on earth. Right? And it was covered in rich green leaves, with fruit on it. And it gave shelter to the animals, and nesting space to all the birds – I mean it was a really great tree.
Daniel	Sounds like it. Go on.
Nebuchadnezzar	There was an angel, right? A great, big, shiny angel, complete with harp, halo and heavenly hairdo – and he came down to the tree. 'Chop it down!' he said. 'Chop off its branches, right? Strip off its leaves, right? And scatter all the animals and birds.' Well, I didn't know what was going on, but I knew it wasn't good. Anyway, he told them to leave the stump in the ground – right? And he had a metal band put round it to stop it rotting, right? And then he got really weird. Started talking about the tree as if it were a person. 'Let him be all wet with dew,' he said. 'And let him live with the animals,' he said. 'And let him lose his marbles completely, and be like an animal himself,' he said. Right? And then he said something about everyone knowing that the Most High is in charge around here. I tell you, it was scary. Right?'
Daniel	[*Aside*] If he says 'right' once more, I'll go mad – right? Oh, no! [*To the king*] You know, I wish this dream was about one of your enemies, Your Majesty, because I really like and respect you. But it's not. It's about you – you're the tree. God thinks you've forgotten who *is* the Most High around here, and you might need taking down a peg or two. Sorry about that, but you're going to have a really hard time. Of course, it might help if you started thinking about others instead of your own glory for a bit.
Narrator	Now, strangely, Nebuchadnezzar didn't take Daniel's

	advice – pity! A year later, he was up on the roof, looking out at the city.
Nebuchadnezzar	Haven't I done well! Other kings do stupid things like going to war, right? I've built cities – with big buildings and tall towers, and stuff – right? I'm the greatest! I'm the Most High!
Narrator	He'd hardly said it before he heard a loud voice.
God	You arrogant pipsqueak! Who d'you think gave you that power in the first place? *I* gave it, and *I'm* taking it away. Learn, Nebuchadnezzar – *learn*!
Narrator	Next thing he knew, he'd changed completely – his hair was long and tangled and his neatly clipped finger-nails grew like claws.
Nebuchadnezzar	I can't be seen like this. I think I'd better get away, right?
Narrator	And that was the last thing he did think for a while – because he forgot how to. He lived like an animal, eating grass, always damp and smelly – even the skunks kept a safe distance. Now, if Nebuchadnezzar had had his wits about him, he'd have known what to do, but he didn't – he'd started to think like an animal, as well as look like one. So it took a long time for the point to sink in. When it did, it was as if someone had turned the light on.
Nebuchadnezzar	This is barmy – comes of getting big ideas, and forgetting who's really in charge around here. OK, God – look, I'm sorry, right? I mean, you're the Greatest – right? The Most High – right? I mean, you're just always going to be at the top – right?
Narrator	At that, King Nebuchadnezzar was transformed again – back to being human, back to the palace, back to things the way they were. Well, almost – there was one important difference. Nebuchadnezzar did an amazing thing. He told his entire story to all his people – every gruesome little detail of it.
Nebuchadnezzar	I'm telling you this, right, so that you can all know who's really in charge around here, right? It's God, right? And he's the big boss, and he's the one we ought to praise – right?
Narrator	Right!!

THREE + ONE: FROM TROUBLE TO TRIUMPH

Give glory to the Lord. (Joshua 7:19)

Colour the dotted shapes to find what Nebuchadnezzar must learn.

These pictures look the same but can you find 6 differences?

58

Week 3: Daniel in the lions' den

Thinking about it

What's the point?

Sometimes it's very tempting to idolise people – especially when there's pressure from others. Giving people their proper respect is important, but sometimes we have to make a stand against idolatry – and sometimes that's a very hard thing to do indeed.

Doing it

Prayer

Loving God,
we're here because you love us
and want us to enjoy being with you.
Help us to learn more about you,
and enjoy being with one another as we do it.
Amen.

From the known to the unknown

Who are the children's favourite pop/film stars? Enjoy the banter that will probably ensue, and keep the conversation positive. Perhaps you might tell them who *your* teenage idols were – that should cause some amusement! It's good to have people we admire, and it's right that people's special achievements are recognised – just as long as we remember that they're mortal, just like us, and they make mistakes. They're not gods!

Tell the story: Daniel 6
(See page 63 for a dramatised version of this story.)

Don't feed the lions

Now, let's be clear. Lions and children don't mix. Just because Daniel did it doesn't mean that playing around with man-eating pussy-cats – or woman-eating ones for that matter – is a good idea. Well, now I suppose I'm going to have to tell you the story.

Daniel was a very important person in the ancient, faraway land of Babylon. There was only the king and one other person above him. And the king really liked Daniel – which upset the junior officials.

One of these people (we'll call him Ben) complained: 'Daniel's a foreigner, and King Darius likes him better than he likes us – and foreigners ought to have all the lousy jobs, not the good ones.' As you can see, stupid prejudice isn't new! Anyway, Ben got a few of his friends together and one of them, Ned, had an idea.

THREE + ONE: FROM TROUBLE TO TRIUMPH

'Daniel always prays to his God three times every day,' said Ned, 'so let's get the king to make a law banning anybody from praying to this foreign God, and then we can get Daniel punished next time he prays.'

'Ooh,' exclaimed Ben, 'that's a good idea. And the punishment will be that he gets thrown to the lions.'

'King Darius would never do that to Daniel,' Ned objected. 'He likes him too much.'

'Don't you know anything?' scoffed Ben. 'In this country, once you've made a law it can't be changed — not even by the king. So once he's signed the law the old fool won't have any choice.'

So Ben and his friends went to see King Darius. 'Your Majesty,' said Ned, 'we think you're a really great king, and we don't like to see you being insulted by people worshipping foreign gods — so we have a suggestion to make.'

Well, King Darius listened and thought it was a great idea. 'I suppose I am rather god-like, aren't I?' he said, vainly. 'All right, then, you write the new law and I'll sign it.'

So the law was passed. Anyone praying to foreign gods would be thrown to the hungry lions as food.

When Daniel heard it, he thought, 'I know what their game is — well, they're not going to stop me praying to the true God, whatever they say.' So that day he did what he'd always done. He went to the window of his room that looked out towards his home city of Jerusalem, and started saying his prayers. And round the corner, watching and listening, were Ben, Ned and their friends. As soon as Daniel started praying, they pounced. They dragged him off to the king and accused him of praying to a foreign God. King Darius was most upset.

'I didn't mean *Daniel's* God,' he protested. 'Honestly, I didn't. Don't worry, Daniel, I'll get you off somehow.' Ben and Ned smiled their evil smiles. They knew the king would have no way out, and would have to throw Daniel into the hungry lions' den.

King Darius tried everything. He checked all the law books, but they all said the same thing. He asked all his advisers, 'Why can't I change the law?' And he always got the same answer.

'That's how we've always done things,' he was told. 'And no one can change the way we've always done things. Not even the king. It's always been like that. We've always done things that way. No one's ever changed anything before.'

Poor Darius. Poor Daniel! 'I'm sorry,' the king said, 'but I've no choice. We'll just have to hope that this God of yours is as clever as you think he is.' So Daniel was led away towards the sound of roaring, ravenous lions bellowing for their food.

King Darius didn't sleep that night — he didn't even drink his cocoa. And as soon as it was light, without waiting for his porridge and his boiled egg, he hurried along to the lions' den. It was horribly quiet. That had to mean just one thing: the lions weren't hungry any more.

UNIT 2: WEEK 3

'Daniel! Daniel! Has your God saved you? Please don't tell me you've been eaten up by the lions!'

The silence seemed to go on for ever. Then Darius heard a voice. 'Morning, Your Majesty. Say "good morning" to the king, Lionel.' And a mighty roar flooded out from the lions' compound. King Darius was overjoyed. 'Open the door!' he shouted to the keeper. 'Get him out! Now!'

God had kept Daniel safe. Amazing! And then King Darius did something that was almost as amazing as that. He changed the law. 'We're all going to worship the God of Daniel from now on,' he said.

His legal advisers were horrified. 'We've never done that,' they said. 'We've always done things our way. We've never done anything like that before. We don't like change. We've never changed anything before.'

'Well,' said King Darius, 'in that case it's about time we did.'

Respond to the story

Discussion

How do the children think Daniel felt when he heard that praying to God had been banned by law?

- Angry?
- Defiant?
- Determined to set a good example to others?

How do the children think he felt when the king sentenced him to be put in the lions' den?

- Glad to have the chance to get closer to nature?
- Absolutely terrified?
- Determined to stand by his principles?

It's probably worth pointing out here that wild animals are dangerous, and just because we're Christians, that doesn't mean we can play with them and not get hurt!

Song

One or more of the following songs might be used here and/or in the all-age worship:

Holy, holy, holy is the Lord
I will wave my hands
Seek ye first the kingdom of God
The King is among us
There once was a man called Daniel

Art and craft

✔ Let the children cut out pictures of famous people – pop 'idols', film stars, politicians, etc. – from magazines and stick them on to a board for display. (This idea is just a variation of the one suggested for Week 1, but since you won't be using both of them in the service that doesn't matter.) Now write the following text in large print on a piece of A4 paper for photocopying:

'Worship the Lord your God, and serve only him.' (It's from Matthew 4:10.) Finally, photocopy the page on to card several times, and cut it up so that each word is on a separate card. You will need enough for each worshipper to be given one. See 'Word and action' in the All-age worship for how this would be used.

Draw or paint a picture of Daniel among the lions.

This is the key picture, but you might want to do others in addition to it, such as:

- Daniel's enemies plotting together
- Daniel's enemies talking to King Darius
- King Darius going to the lions' compound in the morning

Drama

See the opposite page for a dramatised version of the story.

Drama: Don't feed the lions

Narrator	Now, let's be clear. Lions and children don't mix. Just because Daniel did it doesn't mean that playing around with man-eating pussy-cats – or woman-eating ones for that matter – is a good idea. Well, now I suppose I'm going to have to tell you the story. Daniel was a very important person, in the faraway land of Babylon. The king really liked Daniel – which upset the junior officials.
Ben	Daniel's a foreigner – and foreigners ought to have all the lousy jobs, not the good ones.
Narrator	As you can see, stupid prejudice isn't new! Anyway, Ben got a few of his friends together and one of them, Ned, had an idea.
Ned	Daniel prays to his God three times every day, so let's get the king to make a law banning anybody from praying to this foreign God, and then we can get Daniel punished next time he prays.
Ben	Good idea. And for punishment, he gets thrown to the lions.
Ned	King Darius would never do that to Daniel. He likes him too much.
Ben	In this country, once the king's made a law even he can't change it. So once he's signed, the old fool won't have any choice.
Narrator	So Ben and his friends went to see King Darius.
Ned	Your Majesty, we think you're a really great king – and we don't like to see you being insulted by people worshipping foreign gods – so we've got a suggestion to make.
Narrator	Well, King Darius listened and thought it was a great idea.
Darius	I suppose I am rather god-like, aren't I? All right, then, you write the new law and I'll sign it.
Narrator	So the law was passed. Anyone praying to foreign gods would be thrown to the hungry lions as food. When Daniel heard it, he saw exactly what they were up to.
Daniel	I know what their game is – well, they're not going to stop me praying to God, whatever they say.
Narrator	So that day he went as usual to the window of his room, and started saying his prayers. Round the corner, watching and listening, were Ben, Ned and their friends. As soon as Daniel started praying, they dragged him off to the king and accused him of praying to a foreign God. King Darius was most upset.
Darius	I didn't mean *Daniel's* God – honestly, I didn't. Don't worry, Daniel, I'll get you off somehow.
Narrator	Ben and Ned knew the king would have no way out, and would have to throw Daniel into the hungry lions' den. King Darius tried everything. He checked all the law books, but they all said the same thing. He asked all his advisers why he couldn't change the law, and he always got the same answer.

Lawyer	That's how we've always done things, and no one can change the way we've always done things. Not even the king. It's always been like that. We've always done things that way. No one's ever changed anything before.
Narrator	Poor Darius. Poor Daniel!
Darius	I'm sorry, Daniel, but I've got no choice. We'll just have to hope that this God of yours is as clever as you think he is.
Narrator	So Daniel was led away towards the sound of roaring lions bellowing for their food. King Darius didn't sleep that night – he didn't even drink his cocoa. In the morning, without waiting for his porridge and his boiled egg, he hurried along to the lions' den. It was horribly quiet. The lions weren't hungry any more.
Darius	Daniel! Daniel! Has your God saved you? Please don't tell me you've been eaten up by the lions!
Daniel	Morning, Your Majesty. Say 'good morning' to the king, Lionel. [*Sound of lion roaring*]
Darius	Open the door! Get him out! Now!
Narrator	God had kept Daniel safe. Amazing! And then King Darius did something that was almost as amazing as that.
Darius	I'm changing the law. We're all going to worship the God of Daniel.
Narrator	His legal advisers were horrified.
Lawyer	We've never done that. We've always done things our way. We've never done anything like that before. We don't like change. We've never changed anything before.
Darius	Well, in that case it's about time we did.

UNIT 2: WEEK 3

Crack the code to complete the sentence:

King Darius couldn't change the law, but . . .

DANIEL'S GOD SAVED HIM!

| Symbol key: | A | C | D | E | G | H | I | N | O | R | S | T | V | Y |

WORDSEARCH

Find the following words in the grid:
KING, DARIUS, DANIEL, PRAYING, JEALOUSY, GOD, SAVED, BABYLON, LIONS, LAW, CHANGED.

```
B A B Y L O P S A C E D
Z Y T U O L A E J H A W
K I N G M G N I Y A R P
O D A R I U S G S N A D
J E A L O A S Y A G B N
E A N G E D W I V E Y O
A L A T F S A V E D L L
L A R I U S L N R A O Y
O L I O D A N I I N N B
U L I O N S D A N E I A
S I G E A L O U S Y L B
Y B A B Y L O S A V E N
```

65

Week 4: All-age worship

Opening song

A song praising and celebrating the faithfulness of God

Welcome and statement of the theme

Get one or more of the children to point out or hold up the pictures as you sum up the story:

In Junior Church during the past few weeks, we've been learning about how God's people were conquered by the Babylonians and taken into slavery, and how they struggled to be true to God there. We learnt about Shadrach Meshach and Abednego (Who?)*. They refused to bow down to an idol and were thrown into the burning fiery furnace, but God was with them there and the king learnt a lesson. He didn't learn it well enough, though, because the next story was about the king getting a bit too full of his own achievements. He had a dream warning him about pride going before a fall, but he ignored that, and ended up becoming like an animal and living rough. Eventually, he recognised that God was the one who mattered, and he got his throne back. Then we learnt about Daniel – how people tried to stop him praying to God, and he refused to stop – so he was thrown into the lions' den. Once again, though, God was with him – just as he was with Shadrach, Meshach and Abednego (Who?), and the king declared that from now on Daniel's God was the only God people would pray to.

That's the general picture, but today we're going to concentrate on: [*Name the episode of your choice*]

Prayer

– use whichever is appropriate

Based on Week 1

Loving God,
we're here to worship you
and thank you for all the good things you give us.
We enjoy the good things that are around us,
but sometimes they get a bit out of proportion.
Please forgive us when we make idols out of things
and forget you,
and help us always to keep you at the centre of our lives.
Amen.

---

* Prime the children in advance to respond here as they did when you were telling the story.

Based on Week 2

Loving God,
thank you for this wonderful world
you have made for us.
Thank you for all the benefits of science and technology
that we depend on each day.
Please forgive us for sometimes misusing your gifts,
or not realising how they can be misused,
and help us always to keep your love in mind.
Amen.

Based on Week 3

Loving God,
please accept the worship we bring to you.
We know that you are the source
of all meaning in our lives.
Forgive us for sometimes forgetting you
and being distracted by the glitzy things of this world,
and help us to remember that the only true glory
is the glory of your love.
Amen.

Word and action

– use whichever is appropriate

From Week 1

Have the individual word cards given out at random as everyone enters the church. Each person should be given one of each colour.

Now, draw attention to the display and reflect briefly on how easy it is to become idolatrous, just in an understandable attempt not to be different – the trouble being that different is exactly what God calls us to be – as the characters in this story knew.

Have the story read, either in narrative or dramatised form, and then get the congregation to work together – you might find it easier to divide them into groups – to reconstruct the text you have given them. No word is repeated on the same colour of card, so they can start by just swapping duplicates and then see if they can see the text emerging. The first group to finish and assemble the text correctly then come and Blue-Tac their cards over the display of idols. If they get really stuck, tell them where the text is from.

From Week 2

Keeping the second inscription well out of sight, put up the model or flip-chart page and explain that you've erected a monument to science, and you want to inscribe it with the great scientific achievements of the age. You can either divide the congregation into groups at this point to discuss

UNIT 2: WEEK 4

the possibilities, or you can just go ahead and let people call out what they think ought to be on the monument. Don't get into discussion about whether the achievements are unqualified blessings or not until after you have a good number written up.

Now get the discussion going – are these all purely beneficial, or do they have down-sides? Penicillin is one example – over-prescription of antibiotics is causing great concern among doctors who fear our very immune systems are being undermined. Another is genetic engineering – now there's an ethical tangle! Even extending life expectancy is raising dreadfully difficult questions about treatment, geriatric care, and of course the 'switching off' issue – when people's bodies can be kept functioning long after many would say that life in its true sense has ceased.

So while we should celebrate human achievements, we need a corrective to stop us losing our sense of proportion.

Put the second placard over the words 'Science Rocks!' Perhaps that's the corrective – whatever achievements we make have to be used with a recognition of God's purpose in creation. If we lose sight of that, we lose our very humanity.

Here's a story about someone who did just that. Have the story read in either narrative or dramatised form.

From Week 3

Have the individual word cards given out at random as the congregation enter the church.

Now, draw attention to the display and reflect briefly that it's right and proper for people to take pride in their achievements, and we all benefit from having role models and people we admire – just as long as we remember that at the end of the day that's all they are. Sometimes, though, people get carried away by their own propaganda and things get out of proportion. Resisting the pressure to go along with that can be costly, as Daniel found out in the story.

Have the story read, either in narrative or dramatised form, and then get the congregation to work together – you might find it easier to divide them into groups – to reconstruct the text you have given them. No word is repeated, so they can start by just swapping duplicates and then see if they can see the text emerging. The first group to finish and assemble the text correctly then come and Blue-Tac their cards over the display of idols. If they get really stuck, tell them where the text is from.

Song 2

Offering

This may be introduced as a symbol of our commitment to keeping God at the centre of our lives.

Offertory prayer

Lord God,
thank you for always being at the heart of our lives.
Help us to use the gifts you give us
and offer them to you,
so that the world may recognise that, also.
Amen.

Song 3

Reading

Matthew 4:1-11 read from a standard Bible. Introduce it with words such as: Even Jesus was tempted to turn away from God, misuse his power and idolise the ways of the world.

Talk (optional)

If you feel it appropriate (and if time permits), point out that the basic temptations are very similar in all times and places: to allow worldly fame, wealth and power to usurp the true God. Babylon might have won the military battle, but the moral victory was with God's people. And, just in case we start getting the wrong ideas about that, it was *God's* power, not theirs, that won it!

Prayers of intercession

These could be led entirely by the minister or other adult(s), and/or could include some prayers written by the children themselves – or simply some points that they have raised in discussion.

Song 4

Closing prayer/benediction

Unit 3
Jesus: from despair to hope

Overview of the unit

Theme: Jesus shows us God's hope

We take three key events:

Week 1: Simeon's vigil of hope and prayer

Although things seem hopeless, Simeon never gives up hope of seeing God's Messiah, and finally his patience and faith are rewarded.

Week 2: Lazarus is called back to life

Jesus' friend Lazarus dies, but Jesus shows that he is indeed the Lord of life and calls Lazarus back to life in this world.

Week 3: Jesus appears to his disciples at Emmaus

Jesus' friends, distraught at his death, take refuge at home – but the risen Jesus goes with them and, by sharing their journey, their story and their food, helps them to recognise that he is there.

All-age worship

Here, you may choose to focus on any one of the three subthemes, but place it in the context of the overall story and theme: God's faithfulness to his people in distress. So while the specific theme chosen will be emphasised in the choice of 'Word and action' material, some of the art and craft work the children have done in the other weeks will be used to decorate the church and set the context of the wider story.

Important note

✔ The ticked activities in Weeks 1-3 are intended as the link material for the 'Word and action' slot in the all-age worship. You will only need to do this in one of the weeks – depending on which week's subtheme is going to be the main emphasis in the service.

Week 1: Simeon's vigil of hope and prayer

Thinking about it

What's the point?

No matter how desperate things seem to be, God doesn't give up on us. He uses all sorts of people to keep hope alive, or to help bring it to birth – and those who 'only' watch and pray make a vital contribution to that.

Doing it

Prayer

Thank you, God,
for bringing us together again.
Help us to learn about your hope,
and to come to trust you more and more.
Amen.

From the known to the unknown

Can the children remember looking forward to a treat, such as Christmas or a birthday party? Did it seem that the more they thought about it, the longer it took to happen? Sometimes we have to be very patient in our Christian lives – God doesn't always act when we want him to, or in the ways we expect.

Tell the story: Luke 2:21-40

(See page 76 for a dramatised version of this story.)

Never give up hope

Around the time that Jesus was born in Bethlehem, there was an old man living in Jerusalem called Simeon. Although he was sad, Simeon was also full of hope. 'I just know that God's going to do something about all this trouble we're having, before I die,' he used to say. 'God's going to send his special Saviour into the world, and I'm going to live to see it.'

Simeon's neighbours all liked him – you couldn't help liking old Simeon – but, to be honest, they thought he was a little bit dotty. And Maggie, who lived just across the street, was no exception, although she admired him very much.

'I don't know where you get this faith from,' she said to him. 'We've been conquered by the Romans, and their soldiers are everywhere – you can't breathe out of turn without someone telling the governor you're plotting against Rome. Every day, people get tortured to death just for believing something different, and we all know God's given up on us – all of us with any sense, that is.'

'God never gives up,' said Simeon, quietly. 'He always keeps his promises – and he's promised me I'll be around to see it when the Saviour comes.'

'Well, I've got to admire your faith,' said Maggie, 'even if I do think you're crackers. Anyway, I've baked you a few little cakes to cheer you up.'

Simeon smiled. 'Just because I'm old, you think I need cheering up,' he said, 'but you're the one who's saying there's no hope. But thank you, anyway – you're very kind.' Then he stopped for a moment. 'Actually, I'll eat them later,' he said. 'I get the feeling I ought to be at the temple. I think something interesting's happening.'

'Another little message from the Spirit of God, is it?' Maggie laughed, kindly. 'Off you go, then, Simeon – just don't be disappointed, that's all.'

'Oh, don't worry,' Simeon answered, 'I won't be.'

Simeon got to the temple just in time to see a young woman and her husband carrying a baby.

'Hey, look at this, Mary,' the man was saying. 'Just look at the craftsmanship in this cedar chest. I wonder how they get that effect in the carving – I must try it when we get home.'

'Typical!' Mary smiled. 'Even now, you can't get carpentry out of your mind.'

'I'm going to teach Jesus everything I know,' Joseph beamed, proudly.

'Well, let him grow up a bit, first,' Mary laughed. 'And right now, we've got to get him blessed properly.'

Simeon knew these were the people God had brought him here to meet. He just knew, that's all. 'Excuse me,' he said, 'would you mind if I had a look at your baby?'

'Of course not,' Mary answered. 'We're getting used to this – ever since he was born people have been saying how special he is. It's been the most amazing eight days of my life.'

Simeon took the baby from her – very carefully, so as not to drop him. 'Just keep your hand under his head,' Mary advised. 'His neck isn't very strong, yet.'

Simeon looked at the tiny baby. 'So this is the one,' he said quietly. 'Well, Lord, I've waited a long time, but you can let me go now. I can die happy, because I've seen the beginning of your saving work for all nations. This is the one – absolutely, the One! And I've seen him and held him! He's going to bring light into the whole world – and a special kind of glory to your people right here in Israel. Thank you for keeping your promise.'

Then Simeon turned to Mary. 'There are tough times ahead,' he said. 'No quick fix – that's not how God works. This little bundle's going to grow up to change lives – he'll bring joy to a lot of people, but he'll upset some, as well. Sometimes the truth's painful, but that won't stop him telling it. And It won't be any picnic for you, either, I'm afraid.'

Just then an old woman came up. 'This is Anna, a prophet,' said Simeon. 'She's been living day and night in the temple waiting for this moment.'

Anna was almost crying with joy. 'This is the one,' she said. 'This is the Saviour. After all the trouble we've had, God really is doing something. Haven't we always said, Simeon – God keeps his promises?'

Mary and Joseph took Jesus home to their place in Nazareth, where he grew up strong, and wise, and full of faith in God's love for everyone. Even though life was hard, and many people were unhappy, he always had hope. 'God can bring hope out of any amount of trouble,' he used to say. 'Trust me.'

Respond to the story

Discussion

How do the children think Simeon and Anna had felt during all those years of watching, waiting and praying?

- Hopeful?
- Confident?
- Had they sometimes felt impatient?
- Had they perhaps sometimes felt let down when things didn't seem to be happening?
- Might they, perhaps, have been tempted to give up?

How do the children think they felt when they finally saw Jesus?

- Elated?
- Grateful to God?

Song

One or more of the following songs might be used here and/or in the all-age worship:

Be the centre of my life, Lord Jesus
I'm gonna walk by faith
Hang on, stand still, stay put, hold tight
Seek ye first the kingdom of God
There was one, there were two
Watch and pray (Taizé)
We're going to shine like the sun

Art and craft

✔ Make a simple graphic on a flip-chart or whiteboard. (See 'Word and action' in the All-age worship for how this would be used.) Draw a circle, diamond or other shape in the middle and write '(Simeon and Anna) WATCH AND PRAY', making those last three words larger and more prominent than the names. Explain to the children that people who do this are often at the centre of God's saving activity in the world, which is why you've put this in the centre of the page. In the service, the congregation will add the other crucial events of the Christmas story around it.

Draw or paint a picture of Simeon holding the baby Jesus.

This is the key picture, but you might want to do others in addition to it, such as:

- Simeon and/or Anna at prayer
- Mary and Joseph carrying Jesus into the temple

Drama: Never give up hope

Narrator	Around the time that Jesus was born in Bethlehem, there was an old man living in Jerusalem called Simeon. Although he was sad, Simeon was also full of hope.
Simeon	I just know that God's going to do something about all this trouble we're having, before I die. God's going to send his special Saviour into the world, and I'm going to live to see it.
Narrator	Simeon's neighbours all liked him – you couldn't help liking old Simeon – but, to be honest, they thought he was a bit dotty. And his neighbour, Maggie, was no exception, although she admired him very much.
Maggie	I don't know where you get this faith from. We've been conquered by the Romans, and their soldiers are everywhere. Every day, people get tortured to death just for believing something different, and we all know God's given up on us – all of us with any sense, that is.
Simeon	God never gives up. He always keeps his promises – and he's promised me I'll be around to see it when the Saviour comes.
Maggie	Well, I've got to admire your faith, even if I do think you're crackers. Anyway, I've baked you a few cakes to cheer you up.
Simeon	Just because I'm old, you think I need cheering up, but you're the one who's saying there's no hope. But thank you, anyway – you're very kind. Actually, I'll eat them later – I get the feeling I ought to be at the temple. I think something interesting's happening.
Maggie	Another little message from the Spirit of God, is it? Off you go, then, Simeon – just don't be disappointed, that's all.
Simeon	Oh, don't worry, I won't be.
Narrator	Simeon got to the temple just in time to see a young woman and her husband carrying a baby.
Joseph	Hey, look at this, Mary – just look at the craftsmanship in this cedar chest. I wonder how they get that effect in the carving – I must try it when we get home.
Mary	Typical! Even now, you can't get carpentry out of your mind.
Joseph	[*Proudly*] I'm going to teach Jesus everything I know.
Mary	Well, let him grow up a bit, first! And right now, we've got to get him blessed properly.
Narrator	Simeon knew these were the people God had brought him here to meet. He just knew, that's all.
Simeon	Excuse me, would you mind if I had a look at your baby?
Mary	Of course not. We're getting used to this – ever since he was born people have been saying how special he is. It's been the most amazing eight days of our life.
Narrator	Simeon took the baby – very carefully, so as not to drop him.

Mary	Keep your hand under his head; his neck isn't very strong, yet.
Simeon	So this is the one. Well, Lord, I've waited a long time, but you can let me go now. I can die happy, because I've seen the beginning of your saving work for all nations. This is the one – absolutely, the One! And I've seen him and held him! He's going to bring light into the whole world – and a special kind of glory to your people right here in Israel. Thank you for keeping your promise.
Narrator	Then Simeon turned to Mary.
Simeon	There are tough times ahead. No quick fix – that's not how God works. This little bundle's going to grow up to change lives – he'll bring joy to a lot of people, but he'll upset some, as well. Sometimes the truth's painful, but that won't stop him telling it. And it won't be any picnic for you, either, I'm afraid.
Narrator	Just then an old woman came up.
Simeon	This is Anna, a prophet. She's been living day and night in the temple waiting for this moment.
Anna	This is the one. This is the Saviour. After all the trouble we've had, God really is doing something. Haven't we always said, Simeon – God keeps his promises?
Narrator	Mary and Joseph took Jesus home to their place in Nazareth, where he grew up strong, wise, and full of faith in God's love for everyone. Even though life was hard, and many people were unhappy, he always had hope. 'God can bring hope out of any amount of trouble,' he used to say. 'Trust me.'

THREE + ONE: FROM TROUBLE TO TRIUMPH

Lord, my eyes have seen your salvation. (Luke 2:30)

Crack the code to find some good advice for Christians.

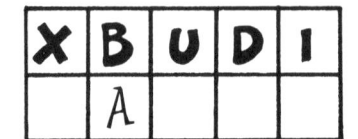

| X | B | U | D | I |
| | A | | | |

| B | O | E |
| A | | |

| Q | S | B | Z |
| | A | | |

Simeon is not alone. Colour the dotted shapes to reveal who is with him.

WORDSEARCH
Find the following words in the grid:
WATCH AND PRAY, SIMEON, HOPE, ANNA, PROPHET, PROMISE, VIGIL, MARY, JOSEPH, JESUS, TEMPLE, SALVATION, SAVIOUR, NAZARETH.

```
P S A L V A T I O N O E
P R O P H A T E M P L E
J V O E M I S A L J P B
E I S M E T E H P O R P
S G I L I I V G H S O R
U I M E O S V I G E E O
S B V I O I E O R P H M
S A L V G M A R Y H E I
S N V I O E R O P H M S
X N L R U O I V A S Y V
Y A R P D N A H C T A W
N A Z A R E T H A T C H
```

Week 2: Lazarus is called back to life

Thinking about it

What's the point?

We need to be careful not to present the *resuscitation* of Lazarus as comparable with the *resurrection* of Jesus. Lazarus came back *from* death to resume his old life – Jesus went forward *through* death to the new! However, we can see it as showing Jesus as Lord of life, and that he wants us to have real life here and now. We don't have to wait for the next world!

Doing it

Prayer

Loving God,
thank you for sharing in our lives,
and wanting them to be as full and satisfying
as they can be.
We thank you for all that we are going to share
this morning,
and ask you to help us know you better, through it all.
Amen.

From the known to the unknown

Do the children know people whose lives are sad? Perhaps they know someone who's lonely because they can't get out very much, or someone who isn't able to make friends. Sometimes that can feel like no kind of life at all – and Jesus wants them to have a life, just as we do.

Tell the story: John 11:1-45

(See page 83 for a dramatised version of this story.)

Get a life, Lazarus

Martha and Mary were friends of Jesus, and they lived with their brother Lazarus at a little town called Bethany, about two miles from Jerusalem.

One day, Lazarus was taken ill. At first his sisters weren't too worried. 'Trust him to catch a cold just as there's housework to be done!' said Martha.

'As far as you're concerned,' Mary answered, 'there's *always* housework to be done.'

'Well, we can't *all* sit around thinking beautiful thoughts all day,' Martha retorted. 'Oh, don't sit on that cushion – I've only just fluffed it up!'

Before long, though, even Martha had to admit that Lazarus had a bit more than a cold. 'We'd better send for Jesus,' she said. 'Now, he'll be hungry when he gets here, so I'll make a few cakes – about five dozen ought to be enough.'

Jesus was with his friends. He was very sad when he heard Lazarus was ill, but he didn't hurry over straightaway. 'We'll go in a couple of days,' he said.

'You'd be mad to go so close to Jerusalem,' Peter objected. 'You know there are people there who are out to kill you – don't you ever learn?'

'What, kill me in broad daylight?' Jesus replied. 'Listen, our friend Lazarus has fallen asleep, and we must wake him up.'

Matthew was amazed. 'You're going to risk your neck to give Lazarus an alarm call?' he said. 'I mean, he's not going to die of too much sleep, now is he?'

'Oh, come on, Matthew,' Jesus answered. 'D'you have to take everything so literally? He *is* dead – *now* d'you get it? It's going to take a little more than an alarm clock to wake him – even if they had been invented, which they haven't. Anyway, it's all working out well – stick with me and you'll see something special.'

The disciples still weren't happy – they thought it was far too dangerous – but Thomas said, 'Have a bit of faith! If he's going to die, let's go and die with him – he'd do that much for us.'

So it was that Jesus and his friends arrived in Bethany, four days after Lazarus died. Martha was busy dusting some daffodils when she heard that Jesus was coming and went to meet him. 'Here you are, at last,' she said. 'If you'd come when we asked you to, Lazarus wouldn't be dead. Still, you're here now, and God will do anything for you, won't he!'

'Your brother's going to rise to life again,' Jesus said.

'Well, yes,' Martha answered. 'On judgement day.'

'When it comes to things like resurrection and life, I'm the one!' Jesus said. 'You do believe that, don't you?'

'Of course – you're the Messiah, Son of God, the One Who Is To Come, all that kind of thing. Look, just wait here while I fetch Mary.'

Jesus waited, and soon Martha came back with Mary.

'Jesus, if only you'd been here,' Mary cried. 'I know you could have saved him.'

Jesus felt really sorry for Martha and Mary, and when they took him to Lazarus' grave he couldn't help crying himself. Some people standing by noticed. 'See how much he loved his friend!' some of them said.

'Oh, terrific!' scoffed someone else. 'He made the blind see, the lame walk, but where was he when his own friend was dying?'

The grave was a hole in the rock, with a big stone rolled in front of it. 'Take the stone away,' Jesus ordered.

'What!' exclaimed Martha. 'He's been dead four days, and there'll be a terrible smell – if that gets into these clothes I'll never be able to wear them again!'

'Didn't I tell you,' Jesus said, 'that you're going to see God's glory in a big way? Now, just have the grave opened and leave the rest to me.'

The stone was rolled back, and the people all around held their noses as Jesus began his prayer to God. 'Father,' he said, 'thank you for listening to me – well, I know you always do, but I have to say that so people here can hear it because they need a bit of convincing that you sent me – you do understand. Right, here we go then.' And he raised his voice to a great shout. 'Lazarus, come out!'

You could have heard a pin drop! Everyone just held their breath – well, they would, wouldn't they, but it wasn't just because of the smell – and waited to see what would happen next. After what seemed like hours, someone said, 'Hey, someone's moving in there!' And out of the darkness of the tomb came Lazarus, still wearing his grave-clothes but very much alive! Everybody started talking at once, full of amazement at what Jesus had done.

'I know he must have been truly dead,' said one. 'No one who's alive smells like that!'

'Jesus must be someone really special, after all!' said another. 'Maybe we should listen to him more.'

Lazarus was still struggling with the grave-clothes. 'Don't just stand there,' Jesus said. 'Set him free, and let him go – he's got a life to live!'

Respond to the story

Discussion

How do the children think Martha and Mary felt when Lazarus came out?

- Overjoyed?
- Amazed?
- Perhaps just a little scared?

We may not be able to raise the dead, but can we help people in other ways to 'get a life'?

- People who are lonely and need company?
- Children at school who don't have many friends, or who get bullied?
- People who are shy and need gentle friendship to give them confidence?

Song

One or more of the following songs might be used here and/or in the all-age worship:

Be still, for the presence of the Lord
Come on and celebrate
Take my hands, Lord
The Spirit lives to set us free
There are hundreds of sparrows
There was one, there were two

Art and craft

✔ Prepare a sign saying 'The Crypt' to go over one of the doors leading off the worship area. (See 'Word and action' in the All-age worship for how this would be used.) Plan which door you will use – preferably, if possible, one which faces the congregation as they sit in their seats. You might want to go further and put a complete façade around the door – it's all a matter of what suits you and your resources. Choose someone – a child or an adult – to play the part of Lazarus in the service. Have a look at 'Word and action' and choose someone you feel will do the part well, but without *over*-playing the comedy.

Draw or paint a picture of Lazarus coming out of the tomb.

This is the key picture, but you might want to do others in addition to it, such as:

- Jesus walking toward Bethany
- Martha and Mary talking to Jesus

Drama

See the opposite page for a dramatised version of the story.

Drama: Get a life, Lazarus

Narrator	Martha and Mary were friends of Jesus, and they lived with their brother Lazarus at Bethany, two miles from Jerusalem. One day, Lazarus was taken ill. At first Martha wasn't too worried.
Martha	Trust him to catch a cold just as there's housework to be done!
Mary	As far as you're concerned, there's *always* housework to be done.
Martha	We can't *all* sit around thinking beautiful thoughts all day, Mary. Oh, don't sit on that cushion – I've only just fluffed it up!
Narrator	Before long, though, even Martha was getting worried about Lazarus.
Martha	Let's send for Jesus. Now, he'll be hungry when he arrives, so I'd better make a few cakes – about five dozen should be enough.
Narrator	Jesus was sad when he heard Lazarus was ill, but he didn't panic.
Jesus	We'll go in a couple of days. Peter, will you tell everybody?
Peter	You'd be mad to go so close to Jerusalem. You know there are people there who are out to kill you – don't you ever learn?
Jesus	What, kill me in broad daylight? Listen, our friend Lazarus has fallen asleep, and we must wake him up.
Matthew	You're going to risk your neck to give Lazarus an alarm call? I mean, he's not going to die of too much sleep, now is he?
Jesus	Oh, come on, Matthew, d'you have to take everything so literally? He *is* dead, and it's going to take more than an alarm clock to wake him – even if they had been invented, which they haven't. Anyway, stick with me and you'll see something really special.
Narrator	The disciples still weren't happy – they still thought it was far too dangerous. But Thomas trusted him.
Thomas	Have a bit of faith, you lot! If he's going to die, let's go and die with him – he'd do that much for us.
Narrator	Jesus and his friends arrived in Bethany four days after Lazarus died. Martha stopped dusting the daffodils and went to meet him.
Martha	At last! If you'd come when we asked, Lazarus wouldn't be dead. Still, you're here now, and God will do anything for you, won't he!
Jesus	Your brother's going to rise to life again.
Martha	I know – on judgement day.
Jesus	When it comes to things like resurrection and life, I'm the one! You do believe that, don't you?

83

Martha	Of course – you're the Messiah, Son of God, the One Who Is To Come, all that stuff. Look, just wait here while I fetch Mary.
Narrator	Jesus waited, and soon Martha came back with Mary.
Mary	Jesus, if only you'd been here, I know you could have saved him.
Narrator	Jesus felt really sorry for Martha and Mary, and when they took him to Lazarus' grave he couldn't help crying himself.
Bystander 1	See how much he loved his friend!
Bystander 2	Oh, terrific! He made the blind see, the lame walk, but where was he when his own friend was dying?
Narrator	The grave was a hole in the rock, with a big stone rolled over it.
Jesus	Take the stone away.
Martha	What! He's been dead four days, and there'll be a terrible smell – if that gets into these clothes I'll never wear them again!
Jesus	Didn't I tell you that you're going to see God's glory in a big way? Now, just have the grave opened and leave the rest to me.
Narrator	The stone was rolled back, and the people all around held their noses as Jesus began his prayer to God.
Jesus	Father, thank you for listening to me – well, I know you always do, but I have to say that so people here can hear it because they need a bit of convincing that you sent me – you do understand. [*Raises voice*] Lazarus, come out!
Narrator	Lazarus came out, still tangled up in his grave-clothes but very much alive! Everybody was full of amazement about Jesus.
Bystander 1	He *must* have been dead – no one who's alive smells like that!
Bystander 2	Jesus must be someone really special, after all! Maybe we should listen to him more.
Jesus	Set Lazarus free, and let him go – he's got a life to live!

UNIT 3: WEEK 2

Which route will lead Lazarus to life?

Lazarus and his friends are celebrating – but can you find 6 differences in the pictures?

WORDSEARCH

Find the following words in the grid:
LAZARUS, MARTHA, MARY, BETHANY, JESUS, GOD, GLORY, THOMAS, DEATH, LIFE, FREE, SAVED, GRAVECLOTHES, MESSIAH, STONE

```
F R E M A R T S U S E J
L A Z A R U S A R F A B
S A V R E E A G I G Z E
T P R T N Y M L A Z A T
O B S H R C O H M Y R H
N H T A E D H A O R U A
E A M D V E T I H O S N
T H O M A E S S T L T Y
G R A V E C D S X G O D
S F R E E S D E A T G E
B E T H A N Y M A R T A
G R A V E C L O T H E S
```

Week 3: Jesus appears to his disciples at Emmaus

Thinking about it

What's the point?

Sometimes people who are finding life tough aren't able to see that Christ is with them. Often it's a simple act of sharing that makes him 'visible'.

Doing it

Prayer

Thank you, Lord Jesus,
for the time that we share here today.
Help us to see that you are sharing in it with us, too.
Amen.

From the known to the unknown

Have the children ever wanted to run away from home? (Virtually all children have threatened to do so at least once!) Perhaps something very upsetting had happened and they needed a bit of space? Here's a story about two people who were so sad when Jesus died that all they could think about was getting away. But Jesus went with them, even though they didn't recognise him!

Tell the story: Luke 24:13-35

(See page 90 for a dramatised version of this story.)

Walking from despair to hope

Cleopas and Judith were friends of Jesus – and they were terribly upset.

'I know Jesus offended a lot of people,' Judith said, 'but they had no reason to have him killed – and in a horrible way like that, as well.'

'He was too honest, that was his trouble,' Cleopas observed. 'Anyway, I don't like Jerusalem any more – let's go home to Emmaus.'

'Good idea,' Judith agreed. 'Let's get away from all these horrible memories.'

So they set out to walk to Emmaus, about seven miles away, and as they walked they tried to make sense of what had happened.

'He was such a good man,' Cleopas said. 'It just doesn't add up.'

'I thought he was the special man God had promised,' Judith added, 'but if he was, why did God let him be killed?'

'Don't look now,' Cleopas whispered, 'but we're not alone.'

He was right – a mysterious figure was catching up with them. 'What are you talking about?' he asked.

Cleopas and Judith stopped and stared. 'You mean, you don't know?'

Judith gasped. 'Are you the only person who's been in Jerusalem this weekend who doesn't know what's happened?'

'Why?' asked the stranger. 'What *has* happened?'

'Oh, nothing much,' sniffed Judith, tearfully. 'They've just gone and killed Jesus, that's all, and after all the wonderful things he did, as well.'

'Yes,' Cleopas added, 'and we were thinking he was the great promised Messiah.'

'That was on Friday,' Judith said, 'and now there are all kinds of rumours going round. Some of our friends went to his grave this morning and came back saying that he'd risen – said they'd seen some angels who'd told them so.'

'Women, you know,' said Cleopas. 'No one else saw anything.'

The stranger spoke kindly, but sounded disappointed. 'When are you going to learn to listen to the prophets?' he said. 'Wasn't all this foretold, that the Messiah would be treated badly, but then God would glorify him?' And before they could stop him he was giving them an off-the-cuff Bible study. They hardly noticed the miles they walked as they listened to him, and before they knew it they were at Emmaus. The stranger was still in full flood, but when they got to their door he stopped. 'Well, I'll say goodnight,' he said.

'Oh, you can't!' exclaimed Judith. 'Look, it's getting dark – why don't you come and stay with us?'

'That's kind of you,' said the stranger, and they went into the house.

'Not much for supper, I'm afraid,' Cleopas apologised. 'We weren't expecting to be home tonight, so the neighbours won't have got anything in for us. We can manage a bit of bread and wine, though.'

'That sounds terrific,' answered the stranger. 'You'd be amazed what you can do with a bit of bread and wine.'

Soon they had a roaring fire going to keep them warm, and the room was beginning to look almost cheerful in spite of everything. They sat down to eat, and Cleopas reached out to take the bread and hand it round, but the stranger got there first. He took the bread, and he said grace, and then, gripping the loaf between his hands he broke it. 'Here you are,' he said. 'Take and eat this.'

Suddenly, a shiver went down Cleopas' spine. It was as though they were back in that room where they'd shared their last supper with Jesus before he'd been killed. Something about the way he said grace . . . and broke the bread . . . and offered it to them. Cleopas looked at Judith, and knew she'd felt it, too. The same tingle, the same flash of recognition. Their eyes met, and lit up with joy. 'It's him!' they chorused, and together they reached out to take Jesus' hands. Laughing and crying at the same time, with joy, they grasped hold of . . . nothing. He wasn't there any more.

'Of course!' laughed Judith. 'He's alive, and he's free, and he's not to be clutched at or held or pinned down by anybody, ever again.'

They didn't say any more, but got up and dashed back to Jerusalem – all seven miles of it. 'This is the place to be!' said Cleopas. 'This is where God's bringing new hope out of all that pain.' And he was right.

Respond to the story

Discussion

How do the children think Cleopas and Judith felt when they thought Jesus was dead?
- Sad?
- Let down?
- Angry?

How do they think they felt when they recognised that he was alive?
- Overjoyed?
- Amazed?
- Suddenly full of life themselves?

Song

One or more of the following songs might be used here and/or in the all-age worship:

Break the bread and pour the wine
Brother, sister, let me serve you
Jesus put this song into our hearts
Walk in the light
We are marching in the light of God
You shall go out with joy

Art and craft

✔ On a number of paper plates write the words 'Jesus is here' – ensuring that the pen you are using is non-toxic! To be doubly safe you could use food colouring, with proper cake-decorating brushes. (See 'Word and action' in the All-age worship for how this would be used.) Explain to the children that it was in the act of sharing that Jesus was recognised, and that's what they are going to remind the congregation about at the service. Then, in time for the service, buy some biscuits to pass round on the plates.

Draw or paint a picture of Jesus meeting his friends on the Emmaus Road.

This is the key picture, but you might want to do others in addition to it, such as:
- Jesus breaking the bread
- Cleopas and Judith running back to Jerusalem
- Cleopas and Judith bursting in on the other disciples with the news

Drama

See the next page for a dramatised version of the story.

Drama: Walking from despair to hope

Narrator	Cleopas and Judith were friends of Jesus – and they were terribly upset.
Judith	I know Jesus offended a lot of people, but they had no reason to have him killed – and in a horrible way like that, as well.
Cleopas	He was too honest, that was his trouble. Anyway, I don't like Jerusalem any more – let's go home to Emmaus.
Judith	Good idea. Let's get away from all these horrible memories.
Narrator	So they set out to walk to Emmaus, about seven miles away, and as they walked they tried to make sense of what had happened.
Cleopas	He was such a good man. It just doesn't add up.
Judith	I thought he was the special man God had promised, but if he was, why did God let him be killed?
Cleopas	Don't look now, but we're not alone.
Narrator	He was right – a mysterious figure was catching up with them.
Jesus	What are you talking about?
Judith	You mean you don't know? Are you the only person who's been in Jerusalem this weekend who doesn't know what's happened?
Jesus	Why? What *has* happened?
Judith	Oh, nothing much – they've just gone and killed Jesus, that's all, and after all the wonderful things he did, as well.
Cleopas	Yes, and we were thinking he was the great promised Messiah.
Judith	That was Friday, and now all kinds of rumours are going round. Some of our friends went to his grave this morning and came back saying that he'd risen – some angels had told them so.
Cleopas	Women, you know. No one else saw anything.
Narrator	The stranger spoke kindly, but sounded disappointed.
Jesus	When are you going to listen to the prophets? Wasn't it foretold that the Messiah would suffer, but then God would glorify him?
Narrator	Before they could stop him, the stranger was giving them an off-the-cuff Bible study. They hardly noticed the miles they walked as they listened to him, and soon they were at Emmaus. The stranger was still in full flood, but when they got to their door he stopped.
Jesus	Well, I'll say goodnight.
Judith	Look, it's getting dark – why don't you come and stay with us?
Cleopas	Not much for supper, I'm afraid – we weren't expecting to be home tonight. We can manage a bit of bread and wine, though.
Jesus	That sounds terrific. You'd be amazed what you can do with a bit of bread and wine.
Narrator	They sat down to eat, and Cleopas reached out to take the bread and hand it round, but the stranger got there first. He took the

	bread, and he said grace, and then, gripping the loaf between his hands he broke it.
Jesus	Here you are – take and eat this.
Narrator	Suddenly, a shiver went down Cleopas' spine. It was as though they were back in that room where they'd shared their last supper with Jesus before he'd been killed. Something about the way he said grace . . . and broke the bread . . . and offered it to them. Cleopas looked at Judith, and knew she'd felt it, too. The same tingle, the same flash of recognition. Their eyes met, and lit up with joy.
Judith and Cleopas	It's him!
Narrator	Together they reached out to take Jesus' hands. Laughing and crying at the same time, with joy, they grasped hold of . . . nothing. He wasn't there any more.
Judith	Of course! He's alive, and he's free, and he's not to be clutched at or held or pinned down by anybody, ever again.
Narrator	They didn't say any more, but got up and dashed back to Jerusalem – all seven miles of it.
Cleopas	This is the place to be! This is where God's bringing new hope out of all that pain.
Narrator	And he was right.

THREE + ONE: FROM TROUBLE TO TRIUMPH

Made known in the breaking of the bread. (Luke 24:35)

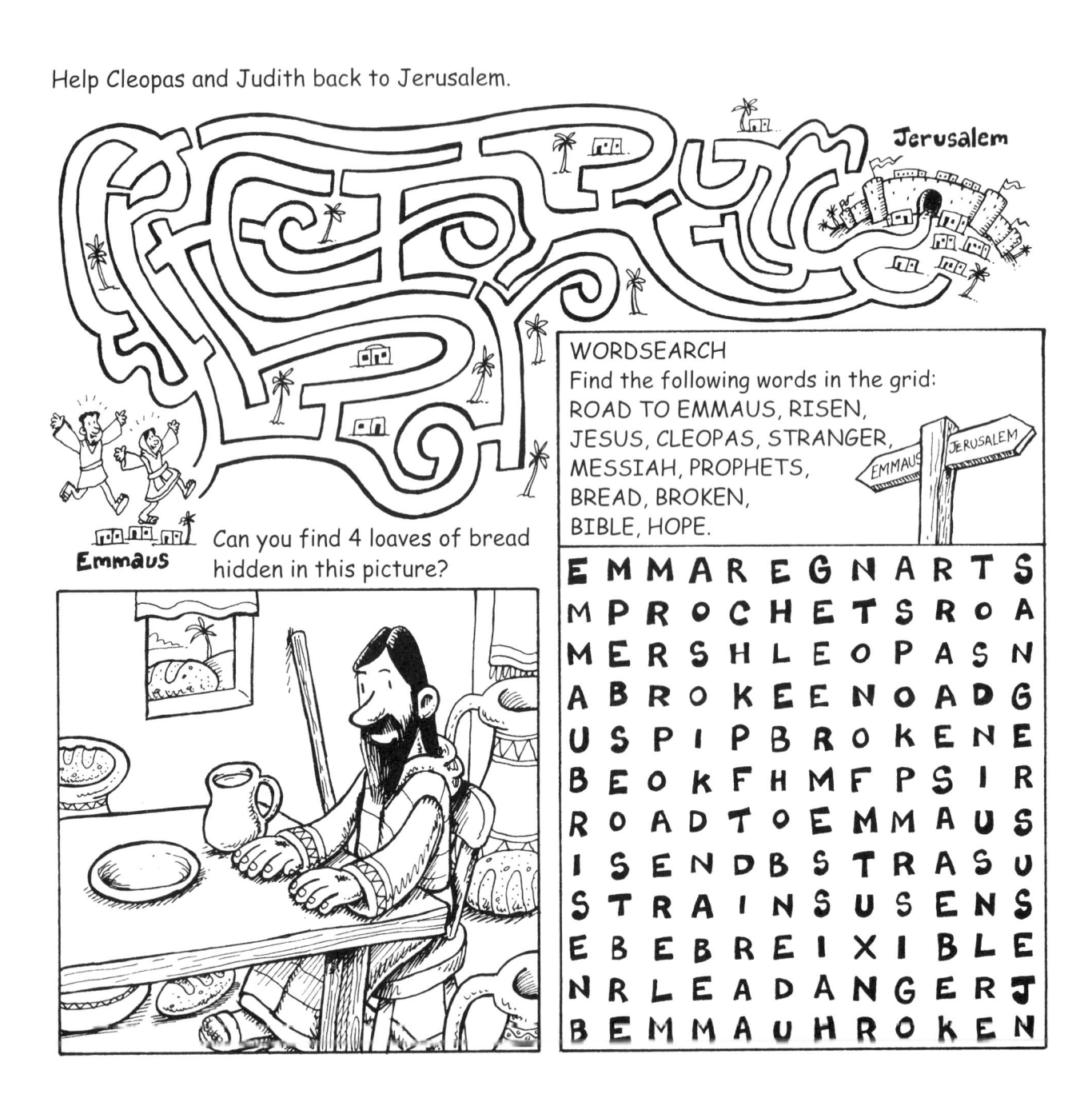

Help Cleopas and Judith back to Jerusalem.

Jerusalem

Emmaus

Can you find 4 loaves of bread hidden in this picture?

WORDSEARCH
Find the following words in the grid:
ROAD TO EMMAUS, RISEN,
JESUS, CLEOPAS, STRANGER,
MESSIAH, PROPHETS,
BREAD, BROKEN,
BIBLE, HOPE.

```
E M M A R E G N A R T S
M P R O C H E T S R O A
M E R S H L E O P A S N
A B R O K E E N O A D G
U S P I P B R O K E N E
B E O K F H M F P S I R
R O A D T O E M M A U S
I S E N D B S T R A S U
S T R A I N S U S E N S
E B E B R E I X I B L E
N R L E A D A N G E R J
B E M M A U H R O K E N
```

92

Week 4: All-age worship

Opening song

A song praising and celebrating the faithfulness of God

Welcome and statement of the theme

Get one or more of the children to point out or hold up the pictures as you sum up the story:

In Junior Church during the past few weeks, we've been learning (more) about God's way of bringing hope out of despair, and the part Jesus played in that. We looked at three stories, beginning with Simeon, the old man in the temple when Mary and Joseph brought Jesus for dedication. We looked at how he'd been watching and waiting, keeping hope alive even when everything around him seemed to say otherwise. Then we turned to the story of Jesus raising Lazarus from the dead, showing himself to be Lord of life and that he wants people to enjoy life in the here and now. Finally, we saw Jesus join the disciples walking to Emmaus on the first Easter Day – sharing their journey, sharing their story and the scriptures, and finally sharing food with them – and we saw how their situation turned from despair to hope and joy when they recognised Christ with them.

That's the general picture, but today we're going to concentrate on: [*Name the episode of your choice*]

Prayer

– use whichever is appropriate

Based on Week 1

Loving God,
we're here not because of our faithfulness,
but because of yours.
We thank you for keeping your promises
to your people down the ages.
Forgive us when we show too little faith in you,
and help us always to pray in hope
and confidence in your grace.
Through Jesus Christ our Lord.
Amen.

Based on Week 2

God of life and love,
we come to worship you
and acclaim you as truly the Lord of life.
We thank you for all that is good
in the lives we live now.
Please forgive us for the times
when our lives don't reflect your love,
and help us to live as true disciples of Jesus
and signs of your love of life.
Through Jesus Christ our Lord.
Amen.

Based on Week 3

Loving God,
we thank and praise you for your love,
stronger than fear and even than death itself.
We thank you for being with your people
even when we don't recognise you.
Forgive us for the times
when our own actions and attitudes obscure your presence,
and help us to live so that others may recognise you.
Through Jesus Christ our Lord.
Amen.

Word and action

– use whichever is appropriate

From Week 1

Have the story read in either dramatised or narrative form and then draw attention to the flip-chart. It looks a bit bare, doesn't it? What else was God doing to prepare for the big event? Get the congregation to call out elements in the Christmas story, for example: Mary is obedient to God; Joseph decides *not* to break up with her; Joseph and Mary go to Bethlehem; Jesus is born; shepherds are told about the birth. Whether you want to be 'theologically correct' and stick just to this Gospel is up to you (and the congregation, who probably won't allow you to anyway!) but the wise men seeing the star could be an apparently faraway event that was still a vital part of the whole.

As these events are called out, write them up on the chart, grouping them around the central motif. Then you can simply reflect back to the congregation that, unbeknown to Simeon and Anna, their watching, praying and waiting vigil was the centre of a growing web of activity all of which contributed to the fulfilling of God's purpose. We can never see all that God is doing at any time, but those who watch and pray – and keep hope alive – fulfil a vital role in it.

From Week 2

The person playing Lazarus will need to either slip out discreetly while the story is being read or wait in the other room for the first part of the service. Have the story read in either dramatised or narrative form and then draw attention to the door. You're going to act out the story now. Call Lazarus to come out, a few times without response. Then turn to the congregation and say you need a bit of help. Could they join in your call? Lazarus could play them along (briefly) by calling out replies such as 'But I've nothing to wear!' and 'Can't I have a shower first?'

When Lazarus emerges, welcome him with applause.

Now you can reflect briefly that many people feel 'entombed' by different things – often a sense of their own unworthiness, or a fear that they will not be welcome or may even be rejected if they venture into places like churches. The church – not just the worship leader or minister! – has a very important role in enabling people to 'come forth' and feel fully a part of this world again.

By this sign, Jesus showed that he is Lord of life and the scourge of death. Perhaps it's not given to many of us literally to bring people back from the grave, but this is a pretty good parallel with it!

From Week 3

Get the children to pass out the biscuits on the specially prepared plates. Ask the congregation to let you know when they get the point of it.

Have the story read in either dramatised or narrative form and then point out to the congregation that Jesus was recognised in the act of sharing.

You can then elaborate further: the two disciples were having a dreadfully troubled time, and thought Jesus wasn't with them any more. Even when he was there, they couldn't recognise him, but *in the act of sharing* his presence was made clear. Maybe there are people today in their position – so troubled that all they can think of is getting away from whatever it is, and unable to see that Christ is walking with them. So who is going to share their journey, their story? And most importantly, who, by sharing friendship, is going to help them recognise that Christ is still with them?

Song 2

Offering

This may be introduced as our contribution to God's mission of hope and redemption.

Offertory prayer

> Loving God,
> we thank you for the rich gifts that you give us,
> and especially for the gift of hope
> in your Son Jesus Christ.
> Here we offer ourselves and our gifts for you to use
> that others may also know your hope.
> Through Jesus Christ our Lord.
> Amen.

Song 3

Reading

Isaiah 30:15-18 read from a standard Bible. Introduce it with words such as: The prophet tells God's people who are in trouble not to panic but to rely on God.

Talk (optional)

If you feel it appropriate (and if time permits) you can sum up the entire unit by saying that God's way of dealing with trouble is to bring hope from within the situation itself – not come riding ostentatiously over the hill like the US Cavalry in a B Western to impose a solution. God doesn't need to come riding over any hills because, whatever the situation, he is already in it!

Prayers of intercession

These could be led entirely by the minister or other adult(s), and/or could include some prayers written by the children themselves, or simply some points that they have raised in discussion.

Song 4

Closing prayer/benediction